IMAGES
of America

MILPITAS

AMERICAN
ELMS

SOUTH/WEST

ALVISO ROAD

237

OLD PENITENCIA
CREEK

CALAVERAS
ROAD

WINSOR BLACKSMITH

GRAMMAR SCHOOL

DR. SMITH/DEVRIES HOUSE

OLD PRESBYTERIAN
CHURCH SITE

S.P.R.R.
CROSSING
THE OLD
OAKLAND
HWY.

JUDGE WELLER'S
DAIRY AND FARM

NORTH

LOOKING SOUTH OVER MAIN STREET, C. 1947. At top, American elms mark the entrance to the John O'Toole Mansion. At bottom is the Joseph Rush Weller dairy and ranch of the 1860s. (Courtesy of Adrian Hatfield Aerial Photography Collection.)

IMAGES
of America

MILPITAS

Robert Burrill
Milpitas Historical Society

ARCADIA
PUBLISHING

Published by Arcadia Publishing
Charleston, South Carolina

Library of Congress Catalog Card Number: 2004109618

For all general information contact Arcadia Publishing at:
Telephone 843-853-2070
Fax 843-853-0044
E-mail sales@arcadiapublishing.com
For customer service and orders:
Toll-Free 1-888-313-2665

Visit us on the Internet at www.arcadiapublishing.com

VARIOUS TRANSLATIONS. Milpitas is a Spanish word derived from *mil* (thousand), and *pitas* (flowers or garden). The name can be translated as "a thousand gardens," "many gardens," and "land of a thousand flowers," according to "Sunshine, Fruit, and Flowers," a souvenir supplement in the *San Jose Mercury News* of 1896. Patricia Loomis cites the Aztec (Nahuatl) word meaning "little cornfields" or "gardens" in her book *Milpitas: The Century of Little Cornfields* (1986).

CONTENTS

ACKNOWLEDGMENTS

This book was completed with the cooperation of many people in Milpitas. In 1969, I was blessed with the opportunity to teach at Samuel Ayer High School in the newly formed Milpitas Unified School District, under the leadership of Superintendent Leo Murphy and administrators Joe House, Jim Brennan, and Bob Nicolai. These role models demonstrated that, through education, the sky is the limit.

The community officially incorporated just 15 years before I came to town. My team included Mabel Mattos, the town historian and the heart of the Milpitas Historical Society, and Velma Valencia, longtime historian and president of the women's club once known as the Bachelor Belles (now known as the Lunch Bunch). These two popular ladies have the great resource of their friends in these clubs. The written sources for this book include the Milpitas Historical Society's scrapbooks, which are filled with significant pictures and articles from the *Milpitas Post*. The primary textbook references are from Pat Loomis and her book, *Milpitas: The Century of Little Cornfields*, published by the Milpitas Historical Society in 1986; and the souvenir edition of "Sunshine, Fruit, and Flowers," published by the *San Jose Mercury News* in 1896. Also, clarification was found in Mort Levine's text *Milpitas: Five Dynamic Decades*.

Individual photo contributors, too numerous to list here, are credited below each caption. Some of the most significant contributors are Jerry Brown, Velma Valencia, Mabel Mattos, Ruth Savage, and Skip Skyrud. Photographs from institutions include those of the Bancroft Library, San Francisco Public Utilities Commission, the San Jose Library, the Dr. Robert Fischer Collection housed at History San Jose, the *Milpitas Post*, the City of Milpitas, the University of Santa Clara, Ed Levine County Park, Milpitas Fire and Police Departments, the Milpitas Chamber of Commerce, the Milpitas Library, and the Milpitas Historical Society. Research was conducted by Velma Valencia, Mabel Mattos, Gabriel Ibarra, Bob Johnson, Jim Reed, Peggy Horyza, Richard Burrill, Jill Singleton, Phil Holmes, Regina Denny, Rob Devincenzi, and Steve Munzel. Bob Chapman gave technical support by keeping my computer and internet connection operating. Hannah Clayborn, Bob Keely, and Steve Munzel were my editors. Encouragement and moral support were provided by friends Bob Chapman, Bob Keely, Velma Valencia, Ernie Wool, and his support-dog Murphy.

I apologize if I have failed to give proper credit where credit is due, or if I provided any incorrect citations. I am especially indebted to those who submitted any information or photos that did not appear in the final product. Your enthusiasm and interest in preserving Milpitas's heritage was appreciated, and I look forward to additional publications and any corrections that might be made. I am very grateful to you all.

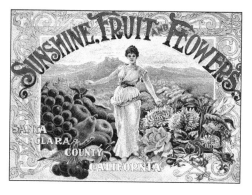

Our history is our heritage, and this compilation is intended to remind the citizens of Milpitas that their heritage is rich and worthy of a permanent archive. Our children and our children's children deserve to know where they came from.

Happy Anniversary, Milpitas!
January 26, 1954–2004.

"SUNSHINE, FRUIT, AND FLOWERS," 1896. (Courtesy of *San Jose Mercury News*.)

INTRODUCTION

The unique history of Milpitas begins in the valleys of the Mount Hamilton Range and the watershed first purchased by the city of San Francisco in 1875. The value of the water and how it was used and managed in the mild and temperate climate of the San Francisco Bay Area provides the stage for our story and explains why so many people wish to live in this "Valley of Heart's Delight."

This book tells the story of the original breadbasket for the Bay Area that became known as the "Valley of Heart's Delight." Once the larger cities of the area became established, there is evidence that Milpitas was left behind, forgotten, and even used as a foil for jokes. Through Arcadia Publishing's *Images of America* series, we are able to reflect upon the essence of "place" through archival photographs. Sandwiched between the covers of this book is a visual record of 50 years of change. As the maps on pages 2 and 128 show, change is inevitable.

Chapter One reveals evidence of our unique natural history in this Bay region. Native Americans were stewards to a natural "Garden of Eden." Chapter Two documents the European and American pioneers who settled here, and the old ways of doing things. In Chapter Three, the reader may be surprised to learn that Milpitas had three railroads. Chapter Four explains the importance of water to this historic breadbasket. Chapter Five commends the humor and humility of the people of Milpitas. Anyone can make a joke about another, but it takes a bigger man to laugh at himself. Chapter Six records the influence of the Ford Motor Company, which rallied the town to incorporate, and the spirit forged and protected by our Milpitas Minutemen. Chapter Seven is a celebration of the last physical hurdle completed, so that Milpitas could become the large city it is today. Here, we also honor our heroes, our war veterans, and our leaders who have inspired us to achieve. Truly, these are the good, the great, and the wise.

The Milpitas Historical Society wishes to dedicate this book to
Elaine and Mort Levine for the record of life they captured over the past 50 years. "With a
camera and a pen, notes and pictures were taken and the Milpitas Post was written."

Thank you for documenting a large part of Milpitas's small-town heritage.
The Milpitas Historical Society honors you.

"HUMILITAS WAS MILPITAS." (Courtesy of Holy Cross Church.)

EXPANSE BETWEEN THE WATERS. "Let there be an expanse between the waters to separate water from the water" (Genesis 1:6). Milpitas is located in the southern part of the San Francisco Bay, where the climate has been described as the best in the world. (Courtesy of author.)

LOWER PENITENCIA CREEK JOINS COYOTE CREEK. The Santa Clara Valley, the "Valley of Heart's Delight," followed the lead of Milpitas, which was the breadbasket for Port Alviso prior to the Gold Rush. Situated within the foothills of majestic Monument Peak above Milpitas, it offered the nearest high point of refuge from seasonal flooding and dependable agricultural produce, supported by a remarkable watershed of natural spring water and artesian wells. Within the Laguna and Calaveras Valleys, this land of a thousand gardens produced more than corn, and it has a history as old as the hills. (Courtesy of author.)

One

IN THE BEGINNING

Thousands of years ago, Native Americans called what was to become Milpitas their home. The San Francisco Bay Area was the center of the largest population in Alta, or Upper California. More than 10,000 Ohlones (Muwekma or Costaños, as they were also called by the Spanish) lived between Big Sur and the San Francisco Bay. They were in place around 400 A.D. Because of the abundant natural resources and a steady climate, the Ohlone's Stone Age lasted approximately 4,000 years. The Ohlone people did not have to develop city-states or farming communities because they were able to manage and live in a comfortable environment with waterways, bays, creeks, and all that they supplied. The hills provided a remarkable watershed.

MOONRISE OVER THE EAST BAY SHORE. This classic photograph, taken from Bayshore Freeway in Palo Alto, illuminates the Mt. Hamilton Range above Milpitas on the right and Fremont on the left. Mission Peak, visible on the left, reaches 2,517 feet. Mt. Allison, in the middle, is 2,658 feet high at its peak. Monument Peak, in the middle-right, is 2,594 feet. This photograph was taken two days before the full moon. (Courtesy of author.)

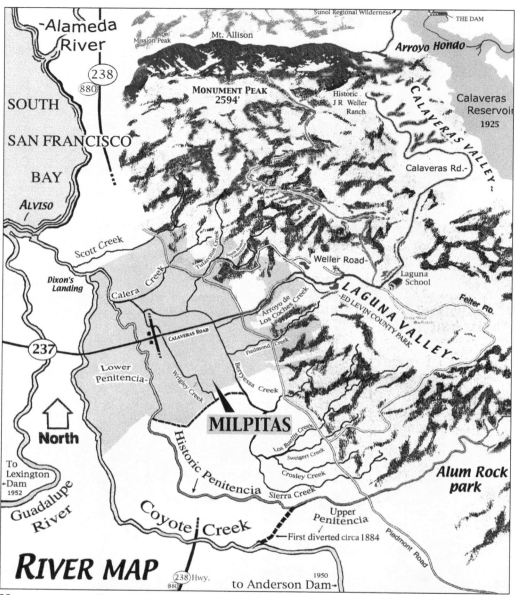

-Alameda River

238
880

SOUTH

SAN FRANCISCO

BAY

ALVISO

Scott Creek

Dixon's Landing

Calera Creek

237

Lower Penitencia-

North

To Lexington -Dam 1952

Guadalupe River

Mission Peak

Mt. Allison

MONUMENT PEAK 2594'

Tularcitos Creek

Wrigley Creek

Arroyo de Los Coches Creek

Piedmond Creek

Beryessa Creek

MILPITAS

Historic Penitencia

Coyote Creek

Sunol Regional Wilderness

Arroyo Hondo

CALAVERAS VALLEY

Historic J.R. Weller Ranch

Calaveras Reservoir 1925

Calaveras Rd.-

Weller Road-

Laguna School

LAGUNA VALLEY

ED LEVIN COUNTY PARK

Felter RD.

CALAVERAS ROAD

Los Buellis Creek

Sweigert Creek

Crosley Creek

Sierra Creek

Upper Penitencia

←First diverted circa 1884

Piedmont Road

Alum Rock park

RIVER MAP

238 Hwy.
880

to Anderson Dam→ 1950

HISTORY AT THE RIVER'S EDGE. "Where there is water, there is life." Milpitas was built along the eastern side of Penitencia Creek in the southeast region of the San Francisco Bay. Ages ago, the Guadalupe River, Coyote Creek, Penitencia Creek, and others joined and formed a giant river that made its way out beyond the Golden Gate, where it emptied into the Pacific Ocean near the Farallone Islands. Between shifting fault plates of the San Andreas and Hayward Faults, a graben basin (a depressed segment of the earth's crust) was formed.

THE OHLONE. Only 300 years ago, there were no horses or wheeled vehicles in the area. People normally did not travel far from home during their entire lifetime although artifacts have been found here from distant places, perhaps indicating trade. Life did not demand the tumult and fast pace that we have grown to know. There were no manufacturers, provisions, and there was nowhere to buy clothing. (Photo by Robert Burrill.)

BOAT MADE WITH TULES. The lightweight tule construction was an important part of the Muwekma hunter-gatherer culture. Tule canoes, housing, watertight basketry, and clothing were all made of this plentiful material. Travel to the local seasonal harvest was essential and explains why heavier ceramic technology is not found in the region. Wildlife was abundant. Elk thrived in the lowlands. Salmon and steelhead ran in many streams. Campfires kept dangerous animals at bay. Only 200 years ago, the grizzly bear was king. (Courtesy of Malcolm Margolin; illustration by Michael Harney.)

INDIAN BEDROCK MORTAR SITE. Behind the Downing Ranch, in the foothills of Milpitas, there is evidence of an earlier time. Ohlone Indian culture here dates back to approximately 1600 BCE. Since their beginning here, as many as 500 generations of Ohlone may have lived at this site. (Courtesy of author.)

SEVEN MORTAR CUPS FOR POUNDING ACORNS. Spring showers temporarily fill the cups. The circle plays an important role in the Indian culture. Acorns, bowls, baskets, the moon, and the sun, all relate to a never-ending cycle through the seasons. Often overlooked, these prehistoric features can be found near a stream or a small spring. (Courtesy of author.)

OAK IN LAGUNA VALLEY. Large oak tree groves were natural orchards in the early California valleys. Time was measured by the oaks. The October acorn harvest marked the beginning of the new year. Winter was spoken of as so many months (moons) after the acorn harvest, summer as so many months before the next acorn harvest. The rhythms of the oak trees marked the passage of the year and defined the rhythms of Ohlone life. (Courtesy of author.)

MORTAR AND PESTLE. For most Ohlone groups, acorns were the staff of life, the food people ate nearly every day of their lives. Unlike wheat, corn, barley, or rice, acorns required no tilling of the soil, no digging of irrigation ditches, nor any other farming. The nutrient value of acorns is extremely high, and is comparable with wheat and barley. Best of all, the acorns were extremely plentiful, and the annual October acorn harvest was held only once each season. These virtues of the acorn help explain why the Ohlone never adopted the practices of agriculture. The preparation of the acorn mush was a woman's daily occupation. The process included gathering, hulling, pounding, and leaching with hot water. The work was not done alone, but with other women. The rhythmic thumping of the women's pestles filled the air. For the Muwekma Ohlone, this was the sound of their village, the sound of home. (Courtesy of author.)

MISSION SANTA CLARA. The eighth mission was founded January 12, 1777, by Fr. Junipero Serra. The first and second log churches were built in 1777 by the banks of Guadalupe River; the third was built in 1784; the fourth in 1818 and 1819. The fifth and current church was built in 1825, remodeled in 1861 and 1887, burned in 1926, and replaced in 1929. This photo was taken on the university campus. (Courtesy of author.)

ROAD MAP TO GOLD. In 1850, there were two ways to the gold fields. The southern route led prospectors by foot down to Mission Santa Clara, east through Milpitas, and up to Livermore, by the way of the Mission San Jose. The other route involved a voyage across the bay and up the Sacramento River, often by steamboat. The golden era of steamboat travel in the San Francisco Bay was from 1850 to 1890. (Courtesy of author.)

MISSION SAN JOSE IN FREMONT. The 14th mission was founded June 11, 1797, by Fr. Fermin Lasuen. The building on the right (above) is a portion of the original mission, and is the oldest building in Alameda County. Earthquakes in 1805 and 1868 left extensive damage with partial restorations in 1916 and 1950. A major renovation of the original chapel was completed between 1982 and 1985. (Courtesy of author.)

MISSION SANTA CLARA MARKER, 1777. (Courtesy of Lou Horyza.)

IMPERIO PORTUGUESE CHAPEL, 1910. Catholic priests from the Mission Santa Clara and the Mission San Jose often met halfway to pray for each other. At first, a small shrine like the Santa Clara mission marker on the left was used, and then a small adobe building, perhaps the size of the Imperio Chapel above was used. They prayed and heard confessions near a small creek that was therefore named Penitencia ("penitence," in English). (Courtesy of author.)

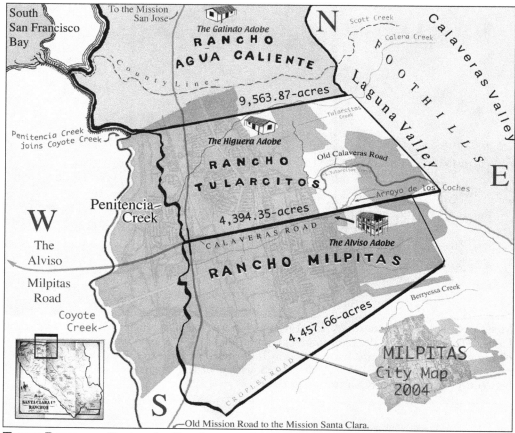

THREE RANCHOS. During the Rancho period (c. 1822–1850), California rancho boundaries were not marked with fences. Landmarks like large rocks, cliffs, gullies, creeks, and rivers were used in most cases. The rancho would be built near a source of water which would later prove to be "Milpitas gold!"

Rancho Agua Caliente (hot water) was the largest rancho, extending four miles to the north from Milpitas at Scott Creek, to a location along the foothills that had a natural warm spring, subsequently the town of Warm Springs. The 9,563-acre parcel was granted by Governor Alvarado in 1839 to Fulgencio Higuera. Juan Crisostomo Galindo participated in the founding of the rancho.

Rancho Tularcitos (little tule thickets) occupied the center of Milpitas, from Calera Creek to the north into the foothills to the east, Los Coches Creek to the south, and Penitencia Creek to the west. The 4,394-acre parcel was granted to José Higuera in 1821 by Pablo Vicente de Sola, the last Spanish governor, and confirmed in 1839 by Gov. Juan Alvarado of Mexico.

Rancho Milpitas (little corn fields or gardens) occupied the south third of Milpitas, bordered with Los Coches Creek to the north, foothills to the east, Berryessa Creek to the south, and Penitencia Creek to the west, where the town of Milpitas was later built. A 4,457-acre parcel was granted to José Maria Alviso in 1835 by the Mexican governor José Castro.

MARIA DE LOS ANGELES ALVISO (1843–1920). Maria was youngest of nine children of José and Juana Alviso, and the last child to be born in the Alviso adobe. (Courtesy of Donna Sepulveda Breitels.)

JOSÉ MARIA ALVISO ADOBE/RANCHO MILPITAS. Original construction of the adobe began in 1840, along the banks of the Arroyo de Los Coches (today's Los Coches Creek). Located on the east side of Milpitas, on Piedmont Road where it ends at East Calaveras Road, the adobe is Monterey style. Thanks to the city of Milpitas, which owns the adobe, a new roof was put on in 1998. New homes surround this city heirloom, and an eight-foot fence secures the grounds. Plans for preservation are being studied. (Courtesy of History San Jose.)

HIGUERA HOTEL RUINS. Rancho Tularcitos, or "little tule thickets," was the name of this land granted to Jose Higuera in 1821. Jose reportedly built this adobe and was probably aided by his son Fulgencio. It still stands today five miles to the north of Milpitas. In this c. 1945 photograph, the original adobe of 1826 is exposed. In 1849, before Clemente Columbet sold the adobe to Henry Curtner, a second level of redwood was added to open a hotel, but the venture was not successful and the building was abandoned. Marion Curtner Weller and Theodore R. Weller, who inherited the ranch, saved the adobe from complete ruin by removing the second floor in the 1950s. Ten years later, the adobe was modernized. (Courtesy of Fremont Museum of Local History.)

HIGUERA ADOBE AND CITY PARK, 1982. Longstanding pepper, fig, and olive trees are preserved in this beautiful city park. In 1970, Marion Curtner Weller gave the adobe and the adjoining land to the city of Milpitas. Portions of the original adobe can still be seen inside the building and through windows built to preserve the infrastructure of the adobe. (Courtesy of author.)

GALINDO-HIGUERA ADOBE. Of the seven adobes on the Rancho Del Agua Caliente, the Galindo-Higuera adobe, located four miles to the north in the Warm Springs district of Fremont, is the only one that remains. Although records dating as early as 1842 associate it with Juan Crisostomo Galindo (pictured here), the actual builder is unknown. Fulgencio Francisco Higuera was granted the land after serving with the Spanish and Mexican governments. Fulgencio shared the pastures and worked together with his father, Jose Loreto Higuera, who earlier had been granted Rancho Tularcitos to the south. As the rancho period waned near the time of the Gold Rush, Fulgencio Higuera and his wife, Marta Clara Saturnina Pacheco, divided the land among their children and sold it to Americans such as Millard, McKeown, and Columbet. Later, Leland Stanford obtained the region for his ranch and winery. (Courtesy of Fremont Museum of Local History.)

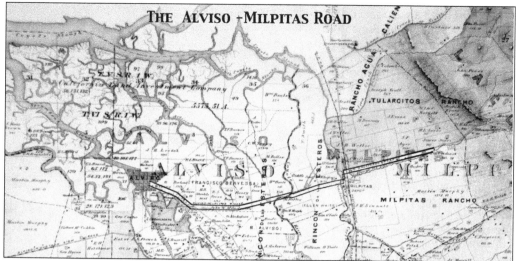

ALVISO-MILPITAS ROAD. After the 1800s, this wagon road became Highway 237 and was the shortest distance around the southern end of San Francisco Bay. The importance of Port Alviso and its nearby farmland of Milpitas cannot be overstated, for it was the "breadbasket" of early Santa Clara County. Farming on the hillsides and valleys of Milpitas provided reliable and profitable crops. Wagons carried produce from the Laguna and Calaveras Valleys to Port Alviso and into San Jose's downtown marketplace. (Courtesy of San Jose Library.)

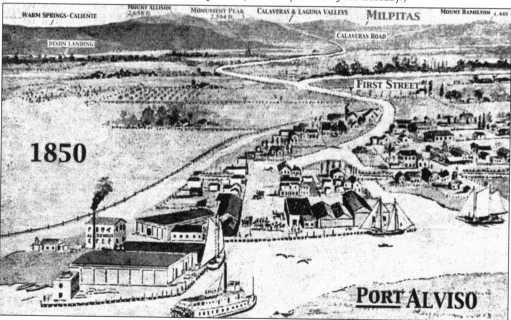

PORT ALVISO. This port funneled supplies and lumber to help sustain Mission Santa Clara (1777) and Mission San Jose (1797), and exported hides, tallow, quicksilver, and agricultural products to other areas. Pioneers were exploring, evaluating, and building the South Bay region. Today, historic Alviso remains a port of entry into the valley's history and contains many interesting buildings, railroad tracks, painted murals, a marina, and the South Bay Yacht Club, known affectionately as the "Blue Lady." (Courtesy of San Jose Library.)

20

ALVISO HARBOR. As early as 1845, mercury from the New Almaden mines was shipped out through Alviso, which was named after Ygnacio Alviso, majordomo at Mission Santa Clara. After 1849, changes resulting from the Gold Rush were profound. Prosperity came to Port Alviso. In 1850, San Jose became the state capitol. Alviso, founded in 1849 and incorporated in 1852, was touted as the "new Chicago of the far West." Initially, Alviso did prosper, although its flat, poorly drained floodplain site limited settlement as flood waters and high tide periodically inundated the frontier town. (Courtesy of *San Jose Mercury News*.)

ALVISO. Steamboat Slough was home to schooners, yachts, barges, houseboats, and scows. The steamship *Alviso* followed in the wake of earlier vessels, but was the pride of the port whose name it carried. This steamer made the daily run from Alviso, leaving at 7:30 p.m. and returning the following morning at 10 a.m. Produce moved at $1 per ton, while passenger fares were 50¢. The *Alviso* (also visible at the upper right, top photo) was built in 1895 and burned in 1920. In 1864, another steam engine—this one on rails—began taking commerce away from the port. By 1869, the railroad was running through Milpitas. (Courtesy of Don L. Dietz.)

DIXON LANDING ROAD ON HIGHWAY 880. Double-masted schooners and flat-bottomed scows once tied up at the crude docks to load hay, grain, and produce from Milpitas and southern Alameda County. Mathew W. Dixon's farm was located close to the Santa Clara County line, where a branch of Coyote Slough lead to Penitencia Creek with a branch called North Coyote. Captain Valpey established a pioneer landing here and built the necessary warehouses. Dixon maintained the landing until the early 1900s.

SWIMMING IN THE BAY. A group of pioneers takes time out to swim at Dixon Landing in this 1885 photograph. The 1868 earthquake collapsed one of the warehouses on the pier, dropped 5,000 sacks of grain into the slough, and knocked the Dixon farmhouse off its foundation. In 1905, Henry Abel bought the deserted two-story Dixon farm house. Then, the house was laboriously dragged by a team of horses two miles to 319 South Main Street, just south of the St. John the Baptist Catholic Church. (Courtesy of Dr. Robert B. Fischer collection, Fremont Museum of Local History.)

Two

HISTORIC MAIN STREET

After 150 years, these magnificent American elms remain the largest noticeable landmark in Milpitas. Standing more than 75 feet tall at the south end of Old Main Street, the elms symbolize strength and resilience. In the 1860s, this was the site of a 100-acre farm that supported a four-story Victorian mansion built by one of the valley's first millionaires. Early on, John O'Toole planted the elms to shade a driveway connecting the mansion to a formal entrance at the south end of Main Street, a quarter of a mile away. Located between Penitencia and Coyote Creeks, the family must have thought that the mound would serve as the best building site, considering the occasional seasonal flooding. But soon thereafter all was not well at the O'Toole estate, despite its elegant appearance. The O'Toole family quarreled and lost their money and had to move. A series of strange misfortunes followed the family for years to come. On the night of April 18, 1906, Thomas Henry O'Toole checked in to Vendome Hotel in San Jose. When an earthquake the next morning collapsed the hotel, he was the only casualty. On October 31, William O'Toole died when his buggy fell off a narrow bridge. For years thereafter, unlucky people were said to have "the bad luck of the O'Tooles." In 1884, Santa Clara County bought the ornate mansion to house poor and elderly citizens. Described by the press as a "poorhouse in a palace," it existed as a home for both the poor and low-risk prisoners until 1957, when county supervisors moved the almshouse operation to another site. The Elmwood property was turned over to the sheriff's department for a new expanded jail, but construction stopped when Native American remains were found at the site.

ELMS LEADING EAST TO MAIN STREET. When John O'Toole began building on the south end of town in the 1860s, Joseph Rush Weller was building his dairy farm on the north end of town. The "Judge" Weller named the town, built the Presbyterian church, and created the Milpitas School District. (Courtesy of Meri Simon.)

VIEW FROM WEST SIDE OF MILPITAS. The grass-carpeted hills of Milpitas shine in the afternoon sun, but as we will see, "there's water in them there hills!" Artifacts from early history were found under the grounds of the Santa Clara County Elmwood Correctional Facility, seen above. Before Elmwood, which took its name from the elms visible on the right, stood the O'Toole mansion. Before that, this was the site of an ancient Indian cemetery. (Courtesy of author.)

Archeologists unearth ancient cemetery at Elmwood construction site

THE MILPITAS POST
1993

by CHRISTINA DALY

Archeologists have unearthed 101 burials and many unique artifacts dating from 1100 to 1500 at the site planned for a new dormitory at Elmwood Correctional Facility.

It has been known since the late 1930s that Elmwood sat on the site of an ancient Indian cemetery, however the number of burials uncovered in the first phase of this project surprised county officials.

"We thought a high estimate for the first phase was 50 to 60 burials," said Cecilia Salazar Arroyo, program manager for Santa Clara County's Capital Programs. "It is much more than any of us first thought."

In addition to the number of burials, Arroyo said the type and condition of burial artifacts found at the site have met federal requirements for being unique discoveries. Among the objects found buried with the dead are carved smoking pipes, whistles made from pelican, swan and eagle bones, intricate beadwork using rectangular shell beads, and sets of charm stones.

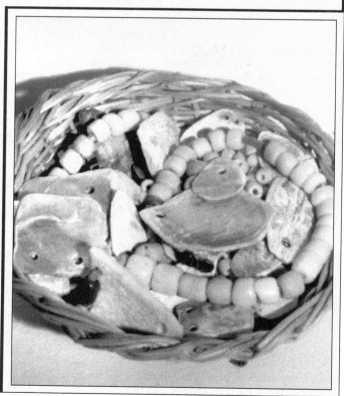

THE OHLONE. The rare effigy ornaments that were found interred with the dead at Elmwood support archeologist Alan Leventhal's belief that "the cemetery was used for very high ranking people." Those ornaments may have looked like the artifacts above.

24

The JOHN O'TOOLE MANSION
Built in 1860

JOHN O'TOOLE MANSION. This beautiful mansion was located where the Elmwood Jail stands today. In 1884, Santa Clara County bought the ornate structure to house poor and elderly citizens, and the building existed as a home for both the poor and low-risk prisoners until 1957, when county supervisors moved the almshouse operation to another site. The Elmwood property was then turned over to the sheriff's department for a new expanded jail. Within the gates of the Elmwood jail community, one small significant structure from the original O'Toole mansion still remains and can be seen on the left side of this photo. Fittingly, the building is being used as the Elmwood Chapel. (Courtesy of San Jose Library.)

FRED GOMES. An immigrant from the Cape Verde Islands, Fred could speak English as well as Portuguese, and was a jack-of-all-trades. Fred lived on Judge R. Weller's dairy, on the north end of town, where he was a foreman and driver for the Wellers. Later in his life he worked as as security guard at the almshouse pictured above. (Courtesy of Joanne Pimentel Souza.)

OLD MAIN STREET, C. 1890. It is presumed that this image faces north on Main Street. Perhaps poles on the street offer clues about the date. According to Alfred Doten's diary, published by the University of Nevada, "The French Hotel burned January 17, 1861, but was immediately rebuilt." Hence, the building on the left may be the Milpitas Hotel, as described on the Sanborn Maps of 1893, and Alviso Road can be seen to the left. (Courtesy of Milpitas Historical Society.)

OLD MAIN STREET, 1900. In this image facing south, St. John's is visible on the right. Just beyond the tree is "the Corner," where Alviso Road reached Main Street from the west. This road leading south was known as the Oakland–San Jose Road or the San Jose–Oakland Road, depending which way you were going. According to the *San Jose Mercury News*, "Early in August 1910, fire destroyed the Milpitas Hotel, three saloons, two barbershops, and a grocery store." Damages were estimated at $25,000, and the heaviest losers were W.W. Parks, Pashote Brothers, Tony Flores, and Frank Terra. This photo was taken just before all the buildings on the right caught fire. (Courtesy of Darlene Thorne.)

OLD MAIN STREET, C. 1912. Comparing another view looking north, two new buildings stand on the left behind the tree that survived the fire, and the street poles have acquired three rows of insulators. The Giacomazzi grocery store is the prominent building on the right. On the left, the first Spanish Mission–style architecture graces the street, built by the Pashote Brothers. (Courtesy of Milpitas Historical Society.)

ST. JOHN THE BAPTIST CATHOLIC CHURCH. The first church built in Milpitas was St. John the Baptist Catholic Church in 1877 at the south end of Main Street. At that time, the population was 80 percent Portuguese. The church was known as San Juan Bautista Church. Sadly, the church burned in 1901, but was immediately rebuilt with a bell tower. (Courtesy of *San Jose Mercury News.*)

27

Main Street Looking north, Catholic Church in foreground, Milpitas, Cal.

SECOND ST. JOHN THE BAPTIST CHURCH, C. 1912. This classic view of the west side of Old Main Street was taken in the same location as the previous picture of St. John's and shows many historic buildings described on the next seven pages. The church's rectory stands closest to the church, followed by the Carlo home and the Carlo store. The last building in sight is the Pashote-Cracolice building, located in the middle of town where Alviso Road ends at Main Street. (Courtesy of Milpitas Historical Society.)

SERVICE AT ST. JOHN THE BAPTIST CATHOLIC CHURCH, C. 1965. Inside the church of St. John the Baptist, a mass is being celebrated for the first communion for local children. Many of the statues and beautiful stained-glass windows still adorn the present St. John the Baptist Catholic Church, located a block west at 360 South Abel Street. (Courtesy of Peggy Horyza.)

CARLO RESIDENCE. The John Rose Carlo residence, built in 1903, is one door north of St John's Catholic Church and conveniently just south of the Carlo store. Standing on the porch is Anna Tomasina Carlo. The baby is Mary Carlo with her parents, Magdalena ("Lena") and John Carlo. Cousin Joseph Laurence Gomes is standing next to the horse. The rider is unknown. From this house, the Carlos could look directly across the street to the Milpitas lumberyard (as seen below) and the railroad station. (Courtesy of Velma Valencia.)

MILPITAS LUMBER COMPANY, C. 1900. Activity abounded on the east side of the street where Manuel Pedro (standing at the door) ran the lumberyard, loading materials onto wagons and railroad cars. In the distance, beyond the freight depot, two boxcars are in view on the Southern Pacific line that ran south to San Jose and north toward Oakland. Notice how high the wagon driver would sit behind the horses. Visibility was important when driving a wagon in traffic. (Courtesy of Joanne Pimentel Souza.)

JOHN R. CARLO STORE. The two photos on this page were taken the same day. In 1908, John Rose Carlo built a grocery store two doors north of St. John the Baptist Catholic Church. That is John Carlo on the left standing with his good friend Mr. Terra, store assistant. First cousin, Joseph Lawrence Gomes, stands to the right. (Courtesy of Velma Valencia.)

GROCERIES, DRY GOODS, AND TOBACCO. Inside, it was a cash-only store, but John Carlo would let farmers charge until they sold their crops for that season. After paying their tabs, the farmers would step out, take off their hats, look up at the sky, and thank God. (Courtesy of Velma Valencia.)

DeSimas Grocery Store. The grocery store, on the east side of Main Street, was owned by Mary Magdelena DeSimas and Joseph Anthony DeSimas. They settled in Milpitas after the Gold Rush. They came from the Sierra boomtown of Rough and Ready in Nevada County. In 1877, they opened one of the first general stores in Milpitas, selling dry goods, spirits, and sundries. Next door in the same building was a shoe repair shop run by Johnny Sylvia, who was known as "Johnny the Shoemaker." There was also a small saloon and a barbershop run by Anthony DeSimas, who was also the barber. (Courtesy of Velma Valencia.)

Candy and a Trim, c. 1925. Rose Dophna and Manuel Pashote sold something everybody needed in downtown Milpitas. Patrons were pampered with a haircut and then indulged with peppermint candy, jawbreakers, and chocolate. They could find out what was going on in town and also walk away with their sweet tooth appeased. (Courtesy of Jerry Brown.)

PASHOTE HOME, MAIN STREET. This large Victorian house was built around 1900 by the Pashote brothers and was the home of Rose and Joe Pashote, who can be seen below at their store across the street. With so many rooms, the house was converted into apartments during World War II. The house is on the east side of Main Street. (Courtesy of Jerry Brown.)

ROSE AND JOE PASHOTE. Conveniently located across the street from their house, under the shade of a palm tree, was the Palm Parlor and Ice Cream Shop. This spot was popular with the local "beaus" and "belles," who would often share the frozen delights the store offered. (Courtesy of Jerry Brown.)

PASHOTE CENTRAL MEAT MARKET, C. 1910. Frank, Joe, Manuel, Jack, Anthony, and John Pashote were all involved in the family enterprise, including the meat market, seen above. Together, these two pages comprise the view from the west side of the street. The Pashote house stood conveniently next door. The Central Meat Market remained the center of town for years to come. The inside of the Central Market is seen below. (Courtesy of Jerry Brown.)

INSIDE THE MEAT MARKET, C. 1916. The sign on the back wall decorated with the American flag reads, "P.P.I.E. or Panama Pacific International Exposition 1915, THE GRAND PRIZE BEEF of the World's Fair, Central Meat Market, The Pashote Brothers, Milpitas, CA." (Courtesy of Velma Valencia.)

FRANK TERRA'S GENERAL STORE AND THE PASHOTE BUILDING, C. 1912. These new buildings are on the west side of the street, across from the Pashote Meat Market. This is the corner (on the left) where Alviso Road ends at Main Street. These buildings replaced the general store, post office, and barbershops that burned in 1910. On the second floor was Maple Hall, a dance floor, and meeting hall for the locals. (Courtesy of Milpitas Historical Society.)

BILLIARDS AND BARBER. In the 1940s, merchants Joe Turturice and barber Jack Goularte offered pool tables and haircuts here. Local folk humor and practical jokes abounded. Every Halloween, barber Jack Goularte suffered through the same prank. Locals got great joy and satisfaction from dragging in a smelly privy and planting it up against Goularte's barbershop door. They just didn't like the way he cut hair! Notice the Fat Boy Barbeque restaurant to the left. It stood at the Corner, serving food and a smile from around 1922 through the late 1960s. (Courtesy of Bob Cracolice.)

34

PASHOTE BUILDING, C. 1915. Spanish Colonial Revival–style architecture was popular from 1915 to 1940. The Pashote building (later "Cracolice") was clearly an example of this style. The building is new, constructed to replace the damage from the large fire of 1910. Notice that the water trough for the horses is still in use. The Victorian street clock on the right can be seen in the picture below. (Courtesy of Bob Cracolice.)

PARKING AT THE HITCHING POST, C. 1915. This crowded scene facing south on Main Street is proof that horses and wagons continued to be used long after the automobile. Notice the power poles above the beautiful Victorian clock and weather vane. That is the Pashote building on the right. The Giacomazzi grocery store (left) was taken down in 1962 and replaced by Milpitas's first shopping center. It was built by the Bettencourt and Madruga families. (Courtesy of Jerry Brown.)

WINSOR BLACKSMITH SHOP. Tom and George Winsor moved from their first blacksmith shop on Carlo Street and built this building in 1922 on North Main Street. Facing west, this building still remains today, without the upper half of the water tank. Their residence, which was located to the rear of the building, is on a street now named Winsor Street. Today, historic artifacts are displayed inside the shop. (Courtesy of Bob Winsor.)

INSIDE THE BLACKSMITH SHOP, C. 1910. Ed and Tom Winsor stand among the tools of their trade. Milpitas smithies developed a reputation for the quality of their craft, and customers came to Milpitas from both sides of the valley. Relative Bob Winsor offered a tip for horseshoes: "A great deal of time was spent upon the design. Corners that were closed in would not let the heat escape and during the branding procedure could produce excessive scarring on the cattle, so a number of alternative patterns were designed." (Courtesy of Bob Winsor.)

JOHN WINSOR'S ROMANTIC TALE. Ill and believed to be near death, John Winsor, seen at right in better health (c. 1850), was left beside the trail in the Utah Territory in the summer of 1852. Nursed back to health by Native Americans, Winsor spent the winter trapping and trading before joining another wagon train heading to California. On the American River, John met a new arrival from his hometown in Iowa who told him his wife had remarried. The bearer of this news was Mrs. Winsor's new husband. Later Winsor met and married an Irish lady named Catherine Costello. Three of their four children were born in the Smith Creek area where they homesteaded. The youngest was Edward Francis Winsor, born in 1863. He founded the Winsor Blacksmith shop operated by his sons, Thomas and George, until the mid-1960s. Other blacksmiths in the Milpitas area were David Boyce, Edward Topham, Ray Madruga, Frank Terra, and Samuel Ayer. Four busy blacksmith shops were all working at the same time. (Courtesy of John Winsor.)

ARTIFACTS OF A BLACKSMITH, 1900. Anything that had to be fashioned in metal was made in the blacksmith shop, using a variety of tools. Inside the Winsor shop, evidence of their handiwork can still be seen. The Winsor smithies would test their designs by branding the wall with each iron. One wall of wooden boards is completely covered with an inventory of their work. The historical society considers these boards a valuable record of the past and plans to identify and preserve them. (Courtesy of Bob Winsor.)

GREEK REVIVAL ARCHITECTURE, 1916. When a fire destroyed the old school house in 1912, the citizens in Milpitas wanted to maintain the high standards of the first school, and so chose to spare no expense. A four-year construction period resulted in this classic grammar school that served area children for 40 years. By 1956, the grammar school had been converted into Milpitas's first city hall and then in 1968, the city expanded and built the first overpass over the railroad tracks to a newer centralized city hall. Currently, a major expansion is being planned that will surround the building on three sides with a new library and will integrate a valued past with a contemporary architectural design. (Courtesy of author.)

SMITH/DEVRIES HOUSE, 1915. At the beginning of World War I, this stately home was built across the street from the classic grammar school. The Dr. Renselaer J. Smith house is the last house of this size from that era that still remains. In 10 years, both buildings will be 100 years old. Gone but not forgotten were the homes of Samuel Ayer, Henry Abel, and Joe Pashote. Although this is not a Frank Lloyd Wright House, it does possess many characteristics similar to the Prairie style. Wright Prairie-style homes were designed to blend in with a flat, prairie landscape with the use of low pitched roofs and overhanging eaves, as seen above. In 1995, the city realized the significance of the Smith/DeVries house and purchased the property for the citizens of Milpitas. (Courtesy of author.)

INTERIOR VIEW, SMITH/DEVRIES HOUSE. The interior Prairie-style architecture incorporated functional, load-bearing interior walls. Rooms were often divided by leaded glass panels. Prairie style, developed by Frank Lloyd Wright and other Chicago area architects, sometimes had custom-designed furniture, and were popular from 1900 to 1920. (Courtesy of author.)

BIG HOLY GHOST QUEEN AND COURT. The queen is Celeste Valencia. The "bar girls" are Phyllis Pedro, Carole Carlo, Joyce Terra, and Hazel Silveria. The "side maids" are Joy Silveria and Regina Duarte. (Courtesy of Velma Valencia.)

"LITTLE" HOLY GHOST QUEEN AND COURT. Fashion was evident in May 1945 at the annual Festa, as dual "queens," young and old, reign over the three day festival. The celebration included a parade to the church for mass and the crowning ceremony, the serving of the "Soupa," an auction, dancing, and fireworks on Saturday night. The "little" queen is Clarence Smith's daughter, Sharron Smith. The "side maids," from left to right, are Bonnie Garcia and Gwen Dutra. The "bar boys," from left to right, are David Rodgers, Danny Rose, Gary Henriques, and Jimmy Rose. The flower girl on the right is Doris Rose. (Courtesy of Velma Valencia.)

Minnie Rose Seimas, Queen Mary Carlo, Mary Soares

PORTUGUESE HOLY GHOST FESTA, 1922. Mary Carlo had a very exciting year. She turned 17 in March, and in May she was queen of the Holy Ghost Festa. Then on the Fourth of July, she was "Miss Liberty" on the Woodmen of the World float. In November, she married Frank "Pop" Valencia at St. John the Baptist Catholic Church in Milpitas. (Courtesy of Velma Valencia.)

HOLY GHOST FESTA, C. 1925. This two-day affair was celebrated on the St. John the Baptist Catholic Church grounds. A few days in advance, colorful flags would decorate the Main Street announcing the festa and the arrival of the carnival. The Grand Marshall (on the right) is John Smith. Lodge members from all over the state would attend each celebration throughout the summer months. The parade is heading south to the church from which this image was taken. (Courtesy of Joanne Pimentel Souza.)

THE S.E.S. PORTUGUESE LODGE. This photo was taken at the St. John's Parish Hall in 1900, the year that the Milpitas S.E.S. Portuguese Lodge was organized. The Lodge was a support group for the Portuguese fraternity. Four persons are identifiable in the picture. From left to right, they are (front row) Manuel Moniz Soares (second from left); Antone Simas (sixth from left); (middle row) John Carlo (seventh from left); (back row) Joseph Vierra Silva (first from left). (Courtesy of Milpitas Historical Society.)

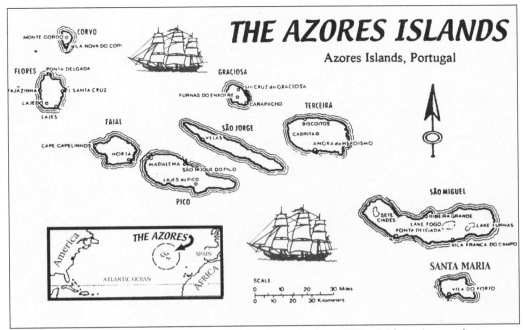

PORTUGUESE MIGRATION. From the 1850s through the 1920s, Milpitas's population was predominately Portuguese. Coming to this country from the Azore Islands, the western islands of Portugal, the young men would hire onto whaling ships and when they got to San Francisco Bay would jump ship to stay in this country. (Courtesy of Velma Valencia.)

HENRY CURTNER, 1831–1916. Mr. Henry Curtner owned land along the foothills from Warm Springs in Fremont to Milpitas. He went out to the docks and recruited the young Portuguese sailors because they knew how to farm on the hillsides and were willing workers. Curtner gave them jobs, places to live, and land for raising food. They became sharecroppers and tenant farmers. They sent for their relatives and then saved up money for their own land, or went into some other type of business. That tradition would continue in Milpitas for generations. The foothills produced wonderful crops of peas, beans, corn, tomatoes, and potatoes, as well as hay. In the early years of agriculture in the Santa Clara Valley, crops were shipped by wagon to Dixon Landing, Port Alviso, and San Jose. Milpitas was a dependable "breadbasket," for the region. (Courtesy of City of Milpitas.)

43

MILPITAS TOWNSHIP. The Honorable Joseph R. Weller (1819–1915), at left, is one of the pioneers of Santa Clara County and Milpitas. He was born in New Jersey, October 10, 1819, and grew up in the state of New York, where he learned to farm. At age 19 J.R. attended Temple Hill Academy and New York State Normal School, graduating in 1846. He worked at an agricultural school and studied law. In 1850, he left for the California gold fields, but by the time he got to San Francisco, he had symptoms of yellow fever. He traveled to the Mother Lode where ill health compelled him to abandon mining prospects and in 1851 he came to Santa Clara County. His health restored, he worked as a tenant farmer on John Murphy's ranch until he was able to buy land at the north end of Milpitas (below). Soon he became involved with the community while growing hay and grain on his new dairy. In 1855, Mr. Weller organized the Milpitas School District and was appointed one of its trustees. In 1856, J.R. was elected to the office of justice of the peace. In 1860, J.R. married Marrion Hart and eventually had two daughters, Marian Elizabeth and May Lucinda. May Lucinda Weller married William Morrison Curtner, which led to the birth of the judge's grandson and granddaughter, William Weller Curtner and Marion Lucy Curtner. (Courtesy of the *Milpitas Post*.)

RAILROAD CROSSING NEAR THE WELLER DAIRY, C. 1876. This drawing accurately depicts north Milpitas, where the road from Oakland crosses the Southern Pacific tracks, past the First Presbyterian Church, and proceeds south along the fence and schoolyard. The farmhouse and dairy belongs to J.R. Weller. At the top is Penitencia Creek that flows into San Francisco Bay to the west. (Courtesy of *Thompson & West Historical Atlas*, 1876.)

At the Scott Creek Ranch. William Weller Curtner and his wife, Ruth Long Curtner, enjoyed their ranch house at the end of Old Scott Creek Road. Mr. Curtner remembered attending the little church as a young boy. But membership dwindled until, in 1915, services were discontinued. The church burned in 1935. (Courtesy of Craighten Jones.)

First Presbyterian Church, 1871–1935. Joseph R. Weller was one of the original founders and organizers of the church, and provided the land at the edge of his ranch on the north end of town . After the church burned in 1935, the bell and the spire at the top of the church were saved by William Weller Curtner (above). In 1967, Mr. Curtner was on the original board that built a new church on Park Victoria on the east side of town. (Courtesy of *San Jose Mercury News.*)

FIRST DOWNTOWN SCHOOL, 1856. The first school in Milpitas was organized by Judge Weller and was held in the first Presbyterian Church (on the left) that doubled as the first schoolhouse. Later, a larger two-story schoolhouse was built (on the right). It burned in 1912. This formal photo was taken on the old Oakland–San Jose Road, which was Old Main Street as it passed through town. At that time, Main Street turned east and then north as it ran very close to the new railroad. (Courtesy of Milpitas Historical Society.)

MILPITAS GRAMMAR SCHOOL, 1953. Josephine Guerrero, Alice Cracolice, Doris Rose, Barbara Gomes, and little Irene Gomes have been recognized in this nostalgic photo. The building is dear to the hearts of many Milpitians. Several generations have attended school at this site. In 1993, the old Milpitas Grammar School building was placed on the National Register of Historic Places, the only site on the city's list granted that distinction. (Courtesy of Ann Mason.)

CLASS OF 1916. This is the first class picture taken on the steps of the old grammar school located at 160 North Main Street, Milpitas, California. The tradition would continue on these steps for another 40 years. Two people have been identified above: Alfred Carlo (on the right side, middle row, third boy from left) and Vernie Miller (front row with hat). The Milpitas Historical Society would welcome more class photos. (Courtesy of Marilyn Dutra Fernandes.)

MORE SCHOOLHOUSES. The Calaveras School and District were first established in 1862 within the Calaveras Valley. The Laguna School (above) and Mission Peak School were added in 1865. This made it easier for students who lived on ranches and farms for miles around to attend. (Courtesy of Milpitas Historical Society.)

SCHOOL DAYS IN THE FOOTHILLS. This is the Laguna School's student body in 1898. Mrs. Gladys Farnsworth Berger of San Jose taught at Laguna from 1931 to 1943 and remembers that "There weren't enough children to keep the school open so I brought my three." Her youngest was the school's only first-grader when Mrs. Berger began teaching. She remembered, "When the little one was taking her nap the other children would be very quiet." One of Mrs. Berger's pupils was Johnny Covo, who was to become a successful rancher. When enrollment declined below the required minimum of five students in 1943, the old school closed its doors. Mrs. Gladys Farnsworth Berger was the last teacher. (Courtesy of Arbuckle collection.)

AIRPOINT SCHOOL. The Airpoint District was formed on March 17, 1903, out of portions of the Laguna and Milpitas Districts. For more than 60 years this classic schoolhouse stood at the entrance to Laguna Valley where Calaveras Road turns at a "T" intersection with Downing Road (today Ed Levin Park). The schoolyard was just above the road where oak trees line the hillside. Today, only the flagpole remains. A short distance up the road a newer, one-room Airpoint School was built in 1966 to replace the older building that had fallen into disrepair. The new building is now used by the school district for special education. (Courtesy of Milpitas Historical Society.)

AIRPOINT SCHOOL, 1914. Schoolteacher Viola Berry (standing at back) was from San Jose. After teaching for a number of years, she left for a short time only to return with her new married name, Viola Tomkin. Grades one through eight were taught for about 45 families that farmed in the Milpitas hills. Janet Silva Childers recalls, "On rainy days, when students could not go out to play, their activity was to take scissors and newspapers in hand and cut out squares for appropriate use in the privies." (Courtesy of Jack Goularte.)

"M" FOR MILPITAS, C. 1922. This patriotic photo was taken within the open patio portion of the grammar school seen on the right. The flags might be held to celebrate a holiday. The students have not been identified, and the Milpitas Historical Society would appreciate your help. In 1922, the Calaveras Dam was still not complete, but the Fat Boy Barbeque had just opened down the street. (Courtesy of Milpitas Historical Society.)

PEARL ZANKER, 1901–1978. Miss Zanker began her long career in 1926, teaching in the only school in Milpitas, the Grammar School at 160 North Main Street. Her grandparents were pioneers in the Alviso region, and Zanker Road remains a signpost of those times. Her father moved to Milpitas to raise his family, and in 1936, Pearl became a teaching principal, a position she held into the 1950s. She then became personnel director in the district office in 1964, where she stayed until her retirement. Pearl Zanker School, located near her former home, was dedicated in 1970. (Courtesy of Ann Mason.)

Three

RAILROAD AND RESERVOIR

There was a lot of excitement in Milpitas on September 6, 1869, when the first train came chugging through town en route from Sacramento to San Jose. Five years earlier, the distant sound of a railroad whistle was first heard to the west, when the San Francisco–San Jose Railroad was built, bypassing Alviso. But on that day, two 12-car Central Pacific passenger trains, each pulled by three locomotives, left Sacramento at 10 a.m. Due to track construction still in progress and celebrations at every town en route, it did not arrive at Niles until 9 p.m. Here, one train went north to Alameda and the other went south to San Jose, so the celebration train passed through Milpitas about 10 p.m. with little or no fanfare. But the first of three railroads had reached Milpitas. Rails became the main transportation route to build the new frontiers, giving the opportunity for freedom and prosperity to those with the courage to move west. Railroad companies in the United States improved upon the British-style locomotives to adapt them for use in the hills and valleys of America. The American railroads were built "on the cheap," conquering all the dynamic contours of our country.

FIRST MILPITAS DEPOT, C. 1875. The depot was located on the west side of the track about 100 yards south of Calaveras Road and Main Street. The station sign reads 41.6 miles from San Francisco on the Southern Pacific Line. That is Alexander Crabb leaning against the semaphore ladder. He was the first stationmaster for Milpitas. The other two and a half are unidentified. (Courtesy of Milpitas Library.)

SECOND STATION ON THE SOUTHERN PACIFIC LINE. This depot was located four blocks south of the first station near St. John the Baptist Catholic Church. The station was a very important community meeting place and place of celebration. Below, the Milpitas Military Band stands for a photo by the baggage and freight office located on the west side of the station. (Courtesy of Darlene Thorne.)

MILPITAS MILITARY BAND, 1920S. On this particular Sunday afternoon, folks enjoyed a band concert. *The Milpitas Post* identified two performers: Frank Amaral on the small tuba and Joe Spangler behind the trombone player. (Courtesy of the *Milpitas Post*.)

TRAIN COMING INTO MILPITAS, C. 1925. Look closely at this romantic image facing north from Calaveras Road. You can almost hear the whistle blowing! (Courtesy of the *Milpitas Post*.)

THE DAYLIGHT 4449. In 1989, this classic locomotive passed through Milpitas on its way south to take part in the filming of the movie *Tough Guys*, starring Burt Lancaster and Kirk Douglas. Many consider this train to be the most beautiful in the world. Orange paint as bright as daylight reflected the golden state of California, and the train traveled every day from Los Angeles to Portland, Oregon. (Courtesy of author.)

CELEBRATING RAILROAD HISTORY. Railroad fans have celebrated the completion of the transcontinental railroad every decade since May 10, 1869. Here, on May 1, 1949, it appears that this ceremonial train was greeted by the entire town of Milpitas! This American type 4-4-0 locomotive was on its way to Oakland and Chicago for another reenactment of the Golden Spike ceremony. Recently discovered in the Roy Graves collection, this remarkable photograph was taken from the roof of the Western Pacific (WP) station (below). Looking toward the southeast, the open space to the left shows how Milpitas appeared in the years prior to the city's incorporation. This Western Pacific station was torn down in the 1950s. (Courtesy of Bancroft Library.)

WESTERN PACIFIC DEPOT, C. 1949. Built after 1925, this Western Pacific station in Milpitas was located near Calaveras Road, just east of Main Street and the SP line. Today, the railroad switching yard fills the space to the right. In his *Prune County Railroading* (1985), Norman Holmes states, "Railroad trivia tells us that when W.P. operated passenger service, the Milpitas station agent was hard of hearing and had a special attachment on the telephone so he could hear the dispatcher!" These tracks passed by the Milpitas Ford plant (not yet visible in the distance) beginning in 1954. Thousands of new Ford cars and trucks were loaded onto trains and shipped throughout the United States. (Courtesy of Roy Graves collection, Bancroft Library.)

NEW WP YARDHOUSE, 1920S. In 1922, the Western Pacific bought five acres of Charles Brandt's 12-acre parcel on Calaveras Road and ran a line in from Niles giving the town two railroads. By 1924, Milpitas had a new rail yard, and the WP began laying additional tracks around the east side of San Jose to access the growing cannery business. Railroad prosperity continues today. (Courtesy of Bancroft Library.)

YARD WHERE TRAINS ARE MADE. In 1953, Ford (visible on the horizon) relocated its Richmond plant and built conveniently between the two Milpitas railroads, the Southern Pacific and the Western Pacific. Today, new automobiles are loaded on to railway cars in Fremont's Nummi plant and rolled into the Milpitas Yard. (Courtesy of author.)

DAM CONSTRUCTION, 1913. As early as 1875, Spring Valley Water Works began purchasing the remarkable watershed above Milpitas. San Francisco had set no limit to its growth, and water became like gold. The breadbasket that fed the pioneers would be transformed, first by teams of horses and then by steam engines. A new railroad would be needed to finish the job. (Courtesy of San Francisco Public Utilities Commission [SFPUC].)

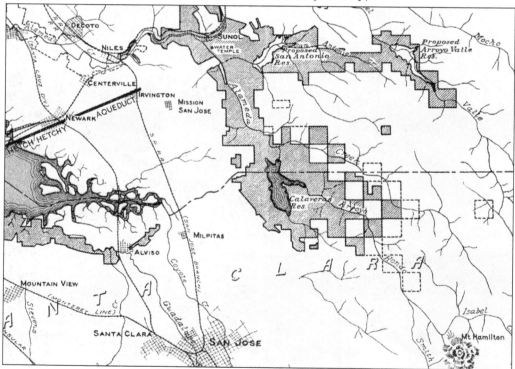

WATERSHED, 1922. From Mount Hamilton (lower right), Smith and Isabel Creeks join and form the Arroyo Hondo, which passed through Calaveras Valley and into Alameda Creek. To locals, the flow of the Alameda Creek appeared endless, but water supplies would become insufficient. (Courtesy of Business Image Group.)

56

WORKING ON THE RAILROAD ON CALAVERAS BOULEVARD, C. 1913. Longtime farmer Joe Cuciz confirmed that "the train went right up Calaveras Boulevard, past his farm, through Laguna and Calaveras Valleys by replacing track from behind to the front of the train." This remarkable photo was recently discovered within Rose Pashote's photo album. (Courtesy of Jerry Brown, Dophna family.)

MAKING THE GRADE. The mobile railroad track was constantly moved on the construction site, to quarry the 2.3 million cubic yards of material. Large, tilting, flat cars were pulled behind a tank locomotive to deposit tons of rock and dirt. At 215 feet high, the dam was to become the largest earth-filled dam in the world. Construction started in 1913 and took 12 years. A series of misfortunes delayed construction. (Courtesy of SFPUC.)

LEGENDARY TOWER. By 1915, a majestic 235-foot tower stood as testimony to the achievement of the dam workers, and as a suggestion of the enormity of what was to come. Construction called for the lower portions to be built up by a hydraulic fill method, and the upper part with a rolled-clay core supported on either side by loosely dumped material containing a large proportion of rock. (Courtesy of SFPUC.)

COMPACTION PROCESS. Slough construction is no longer used today, but was a common practice in early California adobes. The clay was used as a binding agent. Above, thick, muddy water is spilled into deep wheel barrels, which workers dump as directed by the foreman. Compacting the rock fill was very important. Voids in the bulk of the dam could be dangerous. (Courtesy of Mabel Silva Mattos.)

EARTH-FILLED DAM. By Saturday, March 23, 1918, the results of six years of labor could be seen behind the outlet tower. The dam was 1,200 feet long and 1,500 feet wide, but early the next morning the worst happened. There were voids in the fill, and the dam began to slide out and into the tower, pushing it backward, crashing into the lake, and then covering it with tons of rock and dirt. (Courtesy of SFPUC.)

CATASTROPHE, MARCH 24, 1918. The Arroyo Hondo River became a deep creek. It all happened within five minutes. Fortunately, no one was killed. The destruction occurred at sunrise on a Sunday morning as the workers slept in the camp. The dam failed on the south side, with the earth falling back into the reservoir, thereby preventing the water from escaping. However, 600,000 cubic feet of earth had slid from the dam, destroying the floodgate and causing an estimated $500,000 worth of damage. (Courtesy of SFPUC.)

SIX YEARS OF WORK GONE. The front page of the *San Jose Mercury News*'s Sunday paper read, "Calaveras Dam Gives Way; Railroad and Wagons Wrecked; $500,000 LOSS." Thirty-eight wagons and a section of the railroad used in the construction went down among the debris. These remarkable snapshots were taken by Milpitas resident Mathew Vierra Silva, who worked as a watchman at the construction site. (Courtesy of Mabel Silva Mattos.)

CLEAN-UP. Spring Valley Water Company and thirsty San Francisco had to wait another seven years until a new dam was completed. Water from the Yosemite Hetch Hetchy project would not reach the Bay Area until 1930. (Courtesy of Mabel Silva Mattos.)

CALAVERAS DAM, 1925. At 215 feet, the dam holds back the water cycle of the Arroyo Hondo that has percolated down from Mt. Hamilton (4,448 feet) for thousands of years. Hundreds of honeycombed reservoirs have formed deep under the ground, forming artesian wells and natural spring water. This valuable watershed owned by the San Francisco Public Utilities Commission is a water district measuring 139.48 square miles. (Courtesy of SFPUC.)

CALIFORNIA GOLD, C. 1986. Beginning in 2004, the water level of the reservoir was dropped for seismic testing. A new dam—twice the height of the present reservoir—is scheduled for construction within the next 10 years. (Courtesy of author.)

MOUNTAIN FARM OF J.R. WELLER, C. 1896. Ernie Wool knows this beautiful ranch is 2,000 feet above the valley floor because he was raised there with siblings Justin, Betty, Al, and Ruth. It is hard to realize that this ranch site is at the top of the Milpitas hills.

A MODERN VIEW. Standing in the same position as J.R. Weller in the photo above, Ernie Wool explains, "I was fortunate to grow up on this ranch and to have watched this spring continue to flow all my life." Grandson Ted Weller relates that the mineral content found in the water is similar to the water tested in Yosemite. The farm house and the barn may be gone, but the landscape remains the same. This unique watershed is an important part of Milpitas's agricultral heritage.

Four

EARLY AGRICULTURE

Throughout history, more people have been engaged in agriculture than any other occupation. The keys to successful agriculture are the correct preparation of the soil and the availability and application of water. If you could view a cross section of the hills, pictured below, from the top of the watershed to Milpitas, you would see a honeycomb of clear springs that feed a rich soil. This striking panorama was captured more than a century ago. Within these hills and valleys was what fed the "Land of a Thousand Gardens." Chapter four documents, with honor, the agricultural heritage of the Milpitas farmers and their contributions to the early history of the Santa Clara Valley.

VIEW OF THE SOUTHEAST PORTION OF THE SAN FRANCISCO BAY, C. 1896. Looking northward to the city of San Francisco, this shot was taken from the 2,658-foot Mt. Allison, the highest point of the Milpitas Hills. In the middle of the photo, historic Penitencia, Coyote, and Scott Creeks join and form a river that passes through Dixon Landing, crosses Steamboat Slough, and bypasses Port Alviso. The combined rivers meander and become an estuary entering the bay. The *San Jose Mercury News* reporter who took this photo noted, "A long black line of smoke, with a white dot at one end, serves to call attention to a steamboat, which, in the distance, seems to move along most tediously. Long trains, likewise, creep over the plains, followed by a white line of steam and smoke." In the middle of the photo are the hayfields and farmland of the west Milpitas region. (Courtesy of *San Jose Mercury News*.)

HAY BALERS BELOW MILPITAS HILLS. Hay presses were common in the rural areas around the valley when this photo was taken in the summer of 1891. Depending upon the model, the square bails were held together with rope or wire, and weighed between 200 and 280 pounds each. (Courtesy of San Jose Library.)

HAY-BALING COWBOYS. Old-time hay balers worked from sun up to sundown. They ate five meals a day, beginning with a heavy breakfast before the last star fled the sky. After feeding and watering their horses, they ate supper, and then spread their blankets upon "the stack," and literally "hit the hay." (Courtesy of San Jose Library.)

TWO HORSES PULLING HAY. These two handsome horses stand proud on Al Vogel's dairy. Though every country has its own method of haymaking, the principal stages in the process everywhere are (1) mowing, (2) drying or making, (3) carrying and storage in stacks or sheds. (Courtesy of Al Vogel.)

HAY TRUCK ON THE WOOL RANCH. Ernie Wool smiles when he looks at this picture of his "Pappy's" farm truck with all that hay. "That's Pappy (Sandy Wool) standing on the top of the stack. The hay is transported up and into the loft. I can remember Pappy using horses, but driving that truck was one of my fondest memories." (Courtesy of Ernie Wool.)

B&H Ranch, 1986. Built by Alexander and Matilda Rose, the ranch was one of the larger hay and grain operations in the latter half of the 19th century. Hay and grain were fed to the local dairy herds. The early alignment of Calaveras Road traversed northeasterly between the house and the barn, but was realigned to its present position in 1892. Today this classic ranch continues to function as a horse-boarding operation. The barn was built about 1886. (Courtesy of author.)

Cuczi Barn, East of the Alviso Adobe, 1979. In recent years, this barn, built with old growth lumber, was carefully dismantled, and transported to a second historic barn that Joe Cuczi owned a little more than a mile to the north. At the time, ex-mayor Elwood Johnson owned the property, and realized that the wood would best be preserved if used for replacement pieces and for any additions made to another vintage barn. The historic Tank House remains and is one of the last buildings of its kind in Santa Clara County. (Courtesy of author.)

CALAVERAS RANCH ON CALAVERAS RESERVOIR. Danny and Cathy Torres call on Manuel Franco to be the third cowboy when its time for a roundup. Time stands still in the beautiful Calaveras Valley where real cowboys continue the tradition of the 1800s. Before 1913, this valley was a major source of agriculture for San Jose and San Francisco. Wagons loaded with hay and produce traveled to Dixon Landing and Port Alviso. In 1875, the Spring Valley Water Company began purchasing the watershed. They completed the dam in 1924. (Courtesy of author.)

RIDING THE RANGE. Approximately 250 cattle graze the southwest side of Calaveras Reservoir. The San Francisco Public Utilities Commission sponsors the services of these cows and the hands to keep the watershed safe from fire danger. The cows earn their keep by eating the grass, and the hands are asked to keep the cows moving throughout the watershed so that all the grass is mowed. Danny (left) and Cathy Torres also run the ranch, and Manuel Franco rides along on the roundups. (Courtesy of author.)

DOWNING RANCH IN MILPITAS HILLS. George Lucas Downing (1879–1931), below left, purchased land from Henry Curtner and continued the tradition of tenant farming. Like William Weller Curtner, George Downing knew that the Portuguese could farm on the hills and were willing workers. He encouraged the local Portuguese farmers to send for their relatives in the Azores Islands. He would give them a house, a barn, a cow, and a plot of land. Two-thirds of their season's profit would go to the tenant farmer, and the rest would go to Mr. Downing. As many as 30 tenant families farmed the Downing land, very grateful for the opportunity to come to the United States. (Photo of George courtesy of Eleanor Pimentel; photo of ranch courtesy of author.)

COWBOYS AT THE DOWNING RANCH. For the last 30 years, Luis Guzman, from Mexico, has been working the cattle that graze on the steep hills above Milpitas. Local horseman Manuel Franco knows the abilities of this old-fashioned cowboy are legendary. "I saw him pound on the chest of a dying bull that had got tangled up in a barbed-wire fence, and he brought it back to life!" Luis simply responded saying, "Sometimes you have to jump right in there and use your hands." (Courtesy of author.)

WAGON ON THE DOWNING RANCH. In 1921, Joseph Rose and Anton Vierra Silva pose ready to guide a load of dried prunes down Calaveras Road to market. Their destination could be west to the S.P. freight station in Milpitas, south to Market Street in San Jose, or farther west to Port Alviso. (Courtesy of Mabel Mattos.)

VANCE MINNIS WITH "MIKE," C. 1950. At 2,200 pounds, Mike was the darling of the Santa Clara fair and tame as a kitten. Vance Minnis purchased much of the Downing ranch in the Laguna Valley, and with his nephew Jon developed Milpitas Materials, a large cement company in town that provided material for a great deal of the construction in the region. (Courtesy of Ed Levin County Park.)

FIRST DAIRY IN MILPITAS. Established by J.R. Weller in the 1860s, this dairy was located on the north end of Main Street, within sight of the old grammar school, between Penitencia Creek and Railroad Avenue. The Wellers leased the dairy to the Deniz family in the 1940s, and it continued as a working dairy until the 1950s. Milpitas had as many as 10 working dairies over the years. A K-Mart store was built on this property in the 1970s followed by high-density townhouses in the late 1990s. (Courtesy of Alvera "Deniz" Borge.)

WORKING ON THE DAIRY. Children in Milpitas learned about farmwork at an early age. In 1935, Clarence "Sonny" Borges was two years old and helping great-grandpa Luiz Deniz, and by the time he was seven years old, Sonny was milking cows by himself. These photographs were taken by Marion Elizabeth Weller (one of J.R. Weller's two daughters), who lived on the farm most of her life. Sister May Lucinda Weller married William M. Curtner. (Courtesy of Alvera "Deniz" Borges.)

MILKERS. Farmhands earned their name at the Vogel Dairy. Milking machines have revolutionized the process, but back in the 1920s, milking was done the old-fashioned way—by hand. Al Vogel recalls: "The milking schedule began early, at 1:30 in the morning. Breakfast was at 8 a.m. The milkers would work the first 250 cows in about three hours, then alternate positions and do the second 250 cows. Then, at 1:30 in the afternoon, we would do it again, seven days a week!" (Courtesy of Al Vogel.)

TALKING TO COWS. "The milkers would follow the cows into the stanchion stalls where the cow's head was locked into position and fed alfalfa. After a few kind words were exchanged and the shiny, five-gallon bucket was positioned into "udderly" the best position, the milking would begin. We had a couple of five-gallon cows, but three gallons was average. The milk was poured into 10-gallon cylinders, which were closed, lifted, and slid vertically onto a truck that could hold 60 cylinders and 1,200 gallons of milk. I drove the truck and the Golden State Creamery on First Street would receive two deliveries every day." (Courtesy of Al Vogel.)

FRANK AND FERNANDES SERPA DAIRY. The reason for the auction was to retire after 25 years in the dairy business. A dozen dairies operated here in Milpitas. (Courtesy of Serpa family.)

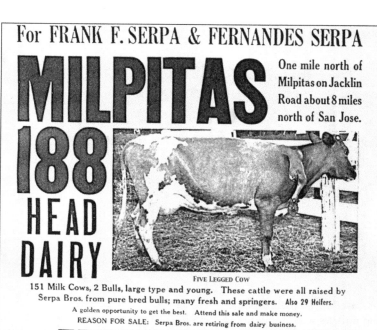

For FRANK F. SERPA & FERNANDES SERPA

MILPITAS

One mile north of Milpitas on Jacklin Road about 8 miles north of San Jose.

188 HEAD DAIRY

FIVE LEGGED COW

151 Milk Cows, 2 Bulls, large type and young. These cattle were all raised by Serpa Bros. from pure bred bulls; many fresh and springers. Also 29 Heifers.

A golden opportunity to get the best. Attend this sale and make money.

REASON FOR SALE: Serpa Bros. are retiring from dairy business.

FRANK J. GOMES

Your Friendly Auctioneer   *For Quick Sale and High Dollar*

Licensed and Bonded

Bayshore Highway and Gish Road   Office Phone San Jose Ballard 5504

FIVE-LEGGED COW. Auctioneer Frank Gomes used this photograph to make people read his poster. The picture was his calling card. He was known as the guy with the five-legged cow! (Courtesy of Serpa Collection.)

TWO-HORSE POWER RIG, C. 1920. Al Vogel Sr. knew exactly how long it would take to harvest an acre of hay. "We would ask the horses. The hay would be laid out in long rows. Then, three farmhands and two large pitchforks were needed to harvest the hay. One slowly drove the horses and wagon along the row, while the second farm hand walked along lifting the hay up and onto the wagon, where the third farmhand stacked the hay. Later, with a tractor, all that fun was taken away." (Courtesy of Al Vogel.)

AL VOGEL'S NEW TRACTOR (INTERNATIONAL TD14). Al Vogel recalls, "When I got my new tractor, I could do in one hour what it took my dad to do in a week!" Al (Junior) Vogel grew up on the dairy (where the *San Jose Mercury News* is now located) and then farmed on the McCarthy Ranch, tilling the fields, on both sides of Alviso-Milpitas Road (Highway 237). (Courtesy of Al Vogel.)

HARVESTING IN THE BREADBASKET, C. 1915. After 1924, Calaveras Valley became a reservoir that provided a primary source of water for San Francisco and became part of the Hetch Hetchy water system. The Wool family was one of the last to farm the historic Calaveras Valley. More than 100 years ago, several pioneer farmers built their homes and were the first to run a plow into this fertile soil, which became the breadbasket of the region. (Courtesy of Wool family.)

PEAS EVERYWHERE. Mabel recalls, "I mean, they planted peas where the goats couldn't go! Then, it was up to us to pick them all!" Up on the hillside, from left to right, are Mabel Mattos, Edward Domingues Silva, Lorraine Borba, and Betty Furtado Silva. (Courtesy of Mabel Mattos.)

BIG CORNFIELDS. The Aztec interpretation of the word Milpitas is "little cornfields," but when you plant corn in Milpitas, it doesn't grow "little!" (Courtesy of Al Vogel.)

APRICOTS. The Louie Gomes family harvested apricots on Evans Road. After the "cots" were picked and cut, they went into large sulphur houses and were smoked to preserve them. The next day they were spread out in the sun to dry. Above, from left to right, are two unidentified workers, and Larry, Irene, and Barbara Gomes. After drying, the apricots were scraped off the tray and boxed to be sent to the packing houses, where they would be packaged and sold at the grocery stores. (Courtesy of Barbara Gomes.)

DRYING APRICOTS. Manuel and Dominic Silva knew that the drying process took a few days, but was dependent upon the sun. (Courtesy of Mabel Mattos.)

LOUIE GOMES, ORCHARDIST. Louie Gomes was a second-generation Portuguese, born in the Santa Clara Valley in 1908, where his family worked as tenant farmers. They saved enough money to purchase 60 acres of hillside between old Jacklin and Evans Roads. There were a dozen Portuguese orchardists living and farming in east Milpitas. (Courtesy of Barbara Gomes.)

FLOWER GROWERS, 1967. Little Winston Chew points to his land of a thousand flowers, where his family first built crude hothouses out of light wooden staves and canvas. This historic image shows rural Milpitas before it was replaced by Interstate 680, which passes north and south through the middle of the city. This large circular parcel (four square miles) was soon surrounded by the beginning of residential development. At this time, however, it was only hay fields and an occasional dairy as far as the eye could see. (Courtesy of Shirley Chew Skruse.)

CHINESE FLOWER GROWERS. Yin Jone Chew came to the United States when he was 10 years old to escape the turmoil of his native China, and began to acquire language, trade, and perseverance that would bring him the rewards of hard work. Arriving in Milpitas in 1956, Yin used his savings of 15 years to buy two acres of hayfield west of Dempsey Road. Soon he began growing flowers. (Courtesy of Shirley Chew Skruse.)

FARMHANDS. Mrs. Helen Chew was in charge of the farmhands: from left to right, Harvey, Winston, and Shirley. Flowers were grown in stages so that new crops would always be visible. Shirley recalls that while in high school she had "no life." Since they created their own seasons, work was year-round. (Courtesy of Shirley Chew Skruse.)

COOKING THE GROUND. Dragging and laying an old anchor chain into position, Harvey secures the plastic tarp for the steam purification machine needed to prepare the soil.

PINCHING IS KEY. Both the number of blooms and the size of the plant are controlled by pinching back the growing tips. When a stem is pinched, the buds at the base of each leaf on that stem are stimulated and begin to grow. A dark canopy was pulled out to increase the "sleep time." Shirley spends countless hours sitting amongst the mums, grooming them to ensure a gorgeous crop. (Courtesy of Shirley Chew Skruse.)

80

MUMS. The chrysanthemum, a member of the *Compositae* family, has been in cultivation in Japan and China for more then 3,000 years. Hybridization in the 1980s brought us the shorter, bushier, bloom-covered domes that are so popular today. (Courtesy of Shirley Chew Skruse.)

LAND OF A THOUSAND FLOWERS. By the mid-1980s, larger manufacturers captured the market, and it was not cost effective for the independent growers to continue. Milpitas is proud of its Chinese growers. The Chew family was one of about seven flower growers once in the vicinity of Milpitas. Today, Highway 680 has replaced the old farming region. (Courtesy of author.)

LOOKING NORTH ON MAIN STREET, C. 1967. Starting at the top, the first horizontal street is Spence Street, which becomes Calaveras Road on the east side of Main Street. Alviso Road enters from the left and ends at Main Street, forming "the Corner." In the middle, Sinnott Laine crosses the tracks and ends at Main Street across from St. John the Baptist Catholic Church. At the lower left is Corning Court and Main Street. The white building at bottom center is Kinney Shoes. The Southern Pacific Railroad freight and passenger station is on the lower right. (Courtesy of Adrian Hatfield Aerial Photography Collection.)

Five

CONTEMPORARY MAIN STREET

Due to the proximity of a series of less-than-gorgeous landmarks, such as a regional dump and a sewage treatment plant—whose pungent odor was carried by prevailing winds from the Golden Gate—Milpitas has received more than its fair share of ribbing over the years. This chapter will set the record straight. Although Milpitas has historically been the subject of fun and jokes, those jokes have brought Milpitas fame and notoriety. And Milpitas may indeed have the last laugh.

VANISHING LANDSCAPE, C. 1950. The only building standing today that can be seen in this photo is the early 20th-century Craftsman-style commercial structure on the right. It was known as Campbell's Corner. (Courtesy of City of Milpitas.)

SMITH'S CORNER FOR 48 YEARS, C. 1940. The Goodwin Hotel was on this corner from 1893 until it burned. When it was rebuilt in 1907, it was renamed after John F. Smith. By 1912, the Smith Corner was a reliable stop for hungry and thirsty travelers, and was home to a long-standing horse trough. The significance of this T-shaped corner cannot be overstated, for this was the crossroads for all travel in the region. The Alviso-Milpitas Road, located at the southern end of the bay, was a main route for travelers from San Francisco. During an earlier era, before bridges, this was the southern route to the gold fields by way of Milpitas to Livermore and beyond. From this familiar point, travelers could also head south to San Jose and on to Carmel and Monterey. (Courtesy of Sharon Smith Briery.)

CAMPBELL'S CORNER. In 1955, Scotty Campbell purchased the Corner and introduced the neighborhood pub motif. The smiling "Scotty" cartoon, under the sign, gave the Fat Boy some company and was integrated into a pink color scheme. The figure in the window was a silver suit of armor that complemented Scotty's golden teeth. (Courtesy of author.)

FAT BOY BARBEQUE, 1975. This Milpitas landmark on the Corner brought a smile to all who passed by on the Old Oakland Road (now Highway 238). Founded in the 1920s, the Fat Boy was one of the first fast food restaurants. The name may have been inspired by movie star Rosco "Fatty" Arbuckle, whose family lived in a house near Airpoint School. The building stood on this corner from the 1920s through the late 1980s. It seemed no one had the heart to tear the little building down. Then, one day, it was hit by a truck. (Courtesy of author.)

MILPITAS ICON. A smile is the key to successful marketing, as this sign, now vanished from the corner, illustrates. Just imagine how many thousands of people smiled back at this fellow on their way through Milpitas. (Courtesy of Robert Chapman.)

KOZY KITCHEN MAKEOVER, 1955. The restaurant was originally the Pashote Meat Market. Beginning July 4, 1945, the Kozy was opened with a partnership between Al and Josephine Carlo and Al's sister Mary and her husband, Frank "Pop" Valencia. The Kozy opened at 4:30 a.m. and closed its front doors at 8:30 p.m. The Kozy was known throughout the region as, "a working man's restaurant," with hot, simple, not-always-good-for-you-but-filling food. Some knew it as the "real" city hall of Milpitas. (Courtesy of the *Milpitas Star*, 1955.)

KOZY KITCHEN RESTAURANT, 1950s. Milkshakes were served up in classic ice cream glasses and were always accompanied by a stainless steel shaker to keep a second helping cold. Sadly, one day this sign was posted: "The Kozy Kitchen is closing January 26, 1999. Our Heartfelt Thanks for Your Friendship & Business for the Last $53^1/_2$ Years. Love and God Bless to All, The Carlo Family." Demolition day was February 18, 2000. (Courtesy of author.)

POST OFFICE. On May 31, 1858, a post office was established in Creighten's store. The name "Milpitas," affixed to the post office, was suggested by Joseph Weller, some early writers claim, as an alternative to "Penitencia," a name some had been using to refer to the crossroads community. Frederick Creighten was the first postmaster, and Joe Weller was the assistant. By 1923, the old Pashote building (at right and on page 35) housed both the post office and a pharmacy and was considered the center of town.

POST OFFICE EXPANSION. In the late 1950s, the building had been purchased and remodeled by Sal Cracolice. Milpitas experienced industrial growth with the new Ford plant, and so an addition was attached to the side of the building, and the first formal post office became visible on the street, seen above. By the early 1960s, a third location was built one block to the north where Calaveras Road crossed the tracks heading east. In the early 1970s, when Calaveras Road was widened and relocated over the railroad tracks, a fourth and more modern post office was built on Abel Street, four blocks to the southwest. A partial list of Milpitas postmasters since 1858 includes Frederick Craighton, Carlos Rose, Ben Rodgers, Josephine Guerrero (unofficial), Walt Eberle, Vincent Cicala, and Terrie Abraham. (Courtesy of the *Milpitas Post.*)

HUMOR AND HUMILITY. Built in 1888, this monumental landmark stood fewer than three miles from Milpitas, and because of its of proximity, it became associated with Milpitas and Alviso. Known as "the Great Asylum for the Insane," the landmark was destroyed in the earthquake of 1906. In 1884, Santa Clara County placed an almshouse for the "old and needy" in Milpitas. By the 1940s, the county started sending prisoners to the almshouse, which became the Elmwood Jail. Soon, the sewage treatment plant was constructed next to the regional dump or landfill. Combined with the prevailing winds that blew in from the Golden Gate, the odor of the salt waters and a variety of agricultural fertilizers created an olfactory phenomenon that could not be dismissed. For many years people riding in cars between the East and the South Bay would make various jocular comments while rolling up their windows as they passed Milpitas. (Courtesy of San Jose Library.)

"AS GOES MILPITAS, SO GOES THE STATE." In 1863, political discussions centered on the Civil War. Rev. Thomas Starr King of the Unitarian church in San Francisco became a major supporter of the Union cause. During one of King's speeches in San Jose, a band of Milpitas citizens must have agreed with his ideas for the future of California, because one man stepped forward and projected onto the wall a lantern slide poster reflecting Milpitans' pride in their community. The message read, "As Goes Milpitas, So Goes the State!" The gesture was well received and attracted attention from the newspapers and the press. The assurance that "the Man from Milpitas would show us the way" was quoted from one end of the state to the other. Satirical vaudevillians in the 1920s remembered the little ditty and found it amusing to think that an educated man would want to live in Milpitas or that Milpitans might lead the state. (Courtesy of San Jose Library.)

BIG BIRD.

GUY SMILEY.

WIN, AND GET A ROUND-TRIP TICKET TO MILPITAS. LOSE, AND GET A ONE-WAY TICKET.

Sesame Street rekindled vaudeville humor about Milpitas

Milpitas Post
Dec. 18 1981

by TOM GILSENAN

FEW PEOPLE I've ever met elsewhere in the US have ever heard of Milpitas. So I'm always pleased to find someone who's heard of our town.

I met one such person in October when I was driving across the country. "Sure, I've heard of Milpitas," she said. "That's the town which used to be a prize on Sesame Street."

To be honest, I'd forgotten about that until she mentioned it. You may have, too.

During the 1970s, Milpitas was regularly mentioned on Sesame Street, the long-running children's program on public television. Our city came up during a segment called "What's My Part," hosted by Guy Smiley.

Smiley, one of the dozens of Muppets created by Jim Henson, gave away trips to Milpitas to other puppets who correctly

Editor's Notebook

identified body parts. Identify a picture of an ear or a nose and the cheery Smiley would award you a trip to Milpitas as a prize.

I"d heard about this long before I saw it. Then one morning my wife, Nancy, called me here at the POST.

Our son, then two, was watching Sesame Street and Guy Smiley was just coming on. "Listen to this," Nancy said, holding the phone up to the TV so I could hear the trip to Milpitas being awarded.

Sesame Street didn't invent the Milpitas prize. Creators of the show borrowed the idea from a turn of the century vaudeville routine. In a comic sketch, the person who cor-

rectly answers a question wins a round trip to Milpitas. Give a wrong answer and you won a one-way ticket to Milpitas.

WHERE vaudeville writers got their idea to use Milpitas isn't clear. Most of those writers lived in New York and never got to California.

One possibility is that writers got the idea from the "As Goes Milpitas" political slogan of the 19th century. Spawned at a political rally in 1862, the slogan came from a sign at the rally which read "As goes Milpitas, so goes the state."

For a time, a measure of political success was how an issue would play with the "man from Milpitas." It was much like the 20th century political measure: "How will it play in Peoria." Perhaps that's where the vaudeville spoof began — poking fun at the man from Milpitas, just as comics today joke about Peoria.

89

LOOKING FOR A BITE TO EAT, 1976. An homage to the giant monster movies of the 1950s, the roots of *The Milpitas Monster* reach back to King Kong and the Japanese Godzilla films. The movie's ecological statement was that man's own waste would return to haunt him. (Courtesy of author.)

DEFENDING AGAINST THE MILPITAS MONSTER. In 1976, Milpitas fire and policeman defended our city from the verbal slings and arrows of sewage plant jokes, or "Noitullop" (pollution spelled backwards), which first attacked our community in 1863. Making our own movie revealed our community's character and pride, as well as our humor and humility. With this model of cooperation and community spirit, it would be well if "as goes Milpitas, so goes the State" were true. (Courtesy of author.)

A Samuel Golden Ayer Production, 1976. The crew of *The Milpitas Monster* included, from left to right, Patti Thorpe, Scot Henderson, Robert Burrill, Andy Watts, and "the Monster," played by Scott Parker. (Courtesy of author.)

World Premiere, May 20, 1976. Cheerleader Krazy George growls like a lion in the film and was on hand for one of the biggest nights in Milpitas history. Search lights, limousines, and the high school band took part in the long-awaited (three years) premiere. Bay Area TV and newspapers helped sell out seats. In October 1976, Congressman Don Edwards published a description of the project in the Congressional Record (Vol. 122, No. 151, part 2) as a model of civic cooperation. (Courtesy of Dwight Caswell.)

FIRST FIREHOUSE, 1947. Located near the Corner of Alviso Road 237 at the Oakland–San Jose Highway, the "Leapin' Lena" fire truck was stored in the Fat Boy Barbeque garage, which was raised and lengthened so that the truck would fit. Tom Evatt recalls: "One day we watched a house burn down and we began taking up a collection to go buy a fire truck." (Courtesy of Milpitas Fire Department.)

VOLUNTEER FIRE DEPARTMENT, 1947. Pictured in the front row, from left to right, are Pete Rogers, Sal Cracolice, Ben Rogers, Manuel Pimentel, and Joe Bettencourt. Posing in the back row, from left to right, are Joe Smith, Clarence Smith, Tom Evatt, Joe and Bill Faria, and Frank Cuciz. Joe Smith, standing at the left, worked across the street at Smith (Campbell) Corner, so he could always reach the fire truck first. That led to him becoming the chief in 1949. (Courtesy of Sharon Smith Briery.)

"LEAPIN' LENA," 1932. GMC "Leapin' Lena" (1947–1956) got her nickname because of the way she would violently lurch forward when the clutch was released. Lena dropped out of sight in the 1960s and was rediscovered by librarian Ed Cavallini in 1992. Bob Keely became a historical society hero as he worked with the Correctional Industries staff who supervised inmates working on the restoration project. It took four years, but all concerned agree it was worth the wait. (Courtesy of author.)

NEW FIRE TRUCKS. In 1953, with a population of 600, a second firehouse was built at the Corner, on the east side of Main Street. Pictured above are a 1956 and 1963 Ford Van Pelt fire trucks, supported by an office, a kitchen-bathroom, and a dorm that sleeps four. In the 1970s, Milpitas began to move into the modern era with its first ladder firetruck, and a third new home on West Curtis, five blocks to the south. Firehouse No. 2, which was once housed in a residence at North Park Victoria and Kennedy Drive, was completed on Yosemite Drive, and firehouse number three was built on Midwick Drive. A fourth firehouse was built in 1993 on the west side of town. (Courtesy of City of Milpitas.)

FIRST FIRE CHIEF, 1947–1971. Joe Smith pioneered local firefighting procedures. Beginning as a volunteer fireman with one fire truck, which sat across the street from his place of work, Joe Smith became aware of the important contributions the fire department had made in the growing community of Milpitas. Joe knew everyone who lived in town and began to recruit others to form the department. Working full time with other fire departments in the area, Joe honed his skills in fire techniques and procedures. Chief Joe Smith trained 35 firemen, purchased five fire trucks, and built a second fire station to the south, near the Ford Plant. Joe retired after 14 years of service, handing the fire department over to Mike Harwood, who had been part of the force in 1968. Fire Chief Mike Harwood served Milpitas for 20 years, bringing the department into the modern era, but clearly the foundation had been laid by pioneer Chief Joe Smith. (Courtesy of the *Milpitas Post*.)

FIREHOUSE NO. 1. In the 1970s, a third station was built on West Curtis Street. This was Joe Smith's final legacy as retiring fire chief. This larger firehouse grew in proportion to the size of the city and was the first to use ladder firetrucks. The department had moved into the modern era as newer equipment and two more firehouses would be opened within the next 10 years. Firehouse No. (seen above) served Milpitas for 20 years before it was replaced with a newer state-of-the-art facility. Today, the new station stands in the same location and is four times larger than the one shown here. (Courtesy of author.)

POLICE CHIEF JIM MURRAY. Beginning in 1957, with only two officers on the force, Chief Murray took over Tom Letcher's badge when he was asked to leave due to a dispute with the city council. Praised for his management skills, Murray set a by-the-book protocol that would be followed by all. Soon, officer candidates were required to have an associate's degree and to be able to pass psychological testing. He liberalized height, weight, and vision requirements, enforced a diverse racial composition of the department, and required high ethical standards. With a growing school population, Murray realized a relationship with students and their curriculum would be essential. Officers were soon acting as liaisons within the schools. Always looking for new programs, Murray became instrumental in developing a canine unit. Dogs were trained, and two selected officers bonded with man's best friend. (Courtesy of author.)

"OFFICERS" GUS, ERIKA, NICK, AND DANNY, C. 1984. These canine "officers" bonded with, from left to right, Shawn Saulsbury, Dan Alday, Archie Labine, and Sharon Johnson. In 1959, Milpitas and Stockton formed the first canine units in California. Since that time, one dog has been on patrol for each of three shifts. (Courtesy of Milpitas Police Department.)

95

MR. MILPITAS, 1907–1999. Sal Cracolice was a bike racer. His last race before he came to Milpitas from San Jose was from San Jose's old city hall up the Peninsula along Crystal Springs to Half Moon Bay and back over the mountain to South San Francisco and south to Bay Meadows race track. His contributions to Milpitas began in the 1928, when he purchased the Pashote building on Main Street. His pharmacy/post office sold the local newspaper, had a public telephone, and sold bus tickets. You could even pay your utility bill there. He was beloved by Milpitians for more than 50 years. (Courtesy of Bob Cracolice.)

RIDING IN SAN JOSE. On the right road, the bicycle is faster than the car.

Six

INDUSTRY AND INCORPORATION

In 1953, land and land prices replaced hay and produce prices as the conversation standbys of the once-sleepy ranch town of Milpitas. Ford officials recognized the advantage of relocating their crowded Richmond plant between two railroads with space to grow. The new 160-acre Ford site was staked for development. The locals were concerned about a tax burden for future industrial construction and they did not want San Jose to tell them what to do. Incorporation was suggested by an East Bay architectural firm and the Western Pacific Railroad. Ford saw advantages to dealing with a local city government rather than dealing with San Jose and its many competing interests. Local merchants John's, Cardoza, Carlo, Rodgers, and Tom Evatt decided to form a city council. Confirmation that the "guest residents" at the county's almshouse and jail could indeed be counted to meet the minimum population requirements of 500 helped to clear the last legal hurdle of incorporation. Campbell's mayor and former city attorney Richard Morton was retained to complete the legal formalities. The young University of California Berkeley graduate Warren Schmid was recommended by the East Bay League of Cities as the first city manager. The Harvard-trained lawyer, Haskell "Jack" Goodman, who was looking to build a part-time practice in Milpitas, became city attorney. January 26, 1954, was the official birthday, and 2004 was the city's 50th anniversary.

FORD PLANT, 1978. In February 1953, Ford vice president L.D. Crusoe said, "The plant will be beautiful to look at. The day of congested industrial areas is over. Plants are now being built out in the open, with lots of room around them. That's the way this plant will be built." (Courtesy of author.)

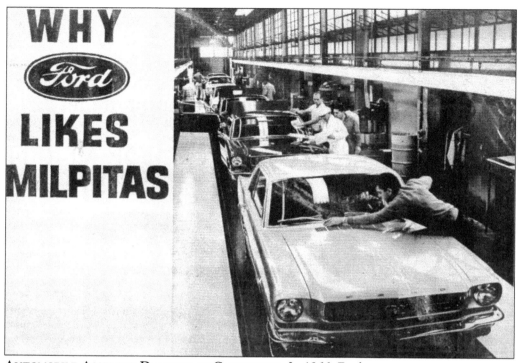

AUTOMOBILE ASSEMBLY DIVISION OF CALIFORNIA. In 1966, Ford wrote

> Eleven years ago, Ford Motor Company selected Milpitas as the Northern California plant. The strategic location of the community, the availability of excellent utilities, the potential it offered good living for our employees, the outlook for continued growth and development . . . these were all things which impressed us. The community has grown and prospered. We are proud of the role played by many of our employees in the city's development. Since the opening of the plant in 1955, we have produced more than ,600,000 Ford cars and trucks to meet the transportation needs of the growing West.

The 1955 four-door model, below, was a popular family car with a spacious backseat for the children. Above, 1966 Mustangs move down the assembly line. The Mustang was very successful for Ford. The standard car cost about $2,400, but with the many options, it could be converted into a hot rod and double in value. (Both courtesy of Milpitas Historical Society.)

And now in 1955. . .

INSIDE THE FORD PLANT. On this site on May 17, 1955, the Ford Motor Company opened the Milpitas assembly plant. At the peak of production, the plant employed 6,000 people producing 55 cars and 22 trucks per hour. The final count was 4,683,679 vehicles when the plant closed 28 years later on May 21, 1983. Above, a small fire was quickly extinguished on the north side of the plant. (Courtesy of Skip Skyrud.)

POWER TO THE PINTO. An optional V-6 engine, offered for the first time in the Pinto station wagon, is installed by workers in Ford Motor Company's Milpitas assembly plant. Light trucks and the Mustang II were also assembled here. (Courtesy of Milpitas Historical Society.)

FIRST CITY HALL, 1954. The local fire district had a little-used office in the fire station fronting on the Oakland Highway where Alviso Road dead-ended. The office was big enough for Warren Schmid, the first city manager, and soon-to-be-hired part-time receptionist Arlene Shaw. Meetings could always be held in the fire station's squad room in the back or in the schoolhouse. After Spangler Elementary School was built, the old grammar school became the first formal city hall. (Courtesy of Milpitas Historical Society.)

ORIGINAL

CITY COUNCIL

FOR THE

CITY OF

MILPITAS

1954

TOM EVATT
Mayor 1954- 56

TOM CARDOZA
Mayor 1956-58

JACK JOHNS
Mayor 1958-60

AL CARLO
Council 1954-62

PETE RODGERS
Council 1954-58

MILPITAS INCORPORATES. On January 26, 1954, Milpitas officially became a city, and was in the running to be one of the wealthiest cities in the area, as its boundaries included the huge $40 million Ford plant. As Milpitas grew up, it learned about big money politics and the continued threat of annexation whereby larger cities could absorb smaller ones. The new city council members would soon be tested. Their first need was to get a low-cost city hall. Besides the small office in the local firehouse, they could use the fire station's squad room or the grammar school. Mayor Tom Evatt ran a motel and was selling real estate. Tom Cardoza was the owner of the Red & White Market. Jack John's ran a mobile trailer park and served on the local school board. Al Carlo was the owner of the Kozy Kitchen Restaurant, which was located in the center of town, a meeting place for the locals and considered by many the heart of the town. Pete Rodgers, the younger brother of postmaster Ben Rodgers, ran a television repair shop. These founding fathers of Milpitas took on a monumental challenge and were willing to learn the old-fashioned way—by doing. (Courtesy of Tom Evatt.)

FIGHTING OFF SAN JOSE.
Annexation by the "bigger
guy on the block" became a
major concern to Milpitas. The
subject of incorporation, first
raised in 1954, was finalized by
a vote on January 23, 1961.

LANDSCAPE CHANGES. This is a San Jose boundary map between 1950 and 1970. Dutch
Hamann had a staff of annexation specialists attached to the manager's office who were tasked
with the growing of the city. Officials in the cities adjacent to San Jose called this the Dutch
Army and they warned that it never slept. San Jose's map of its own city limits during the 1960s
resembled an octopus with dozens of recently annexed tentacles extending in every direction.
(Courtesy of Mort Levine.)

"M" IS BIG IN MILPITAS. Milpitas remembers the patriotic actions of Denny Weisgerber and John McDermott. Like Paul Revere, these good neighbors rallied the citizens to action with the introduction of the Milpitas Minutemen. In 1961, a group with close ties to disgruntled developers and San Jose city officials still upset that they had lost the Ford Plant to Milpitas, advanced with a surprise advertising campaign to force a vote annexing Milpitas. Milpitas needed a defense and they needed it now! Headquarters became Denny Weisgerber's house; after all, his symbolic phone number was 262-1776. (Courtesy of author.)

John McDermott commissioned Joe Brown to paint a patriotic symbol literally overnight. Four thousand decals were printed and distributed the very next day. The troops had been rallied, and the vote came in at 1,571 to 395. Citizens were unified and a new city secured. John and his wife, Betty, moved to Casper Street in 1956. In the 1960s, McDermott was elected to the city council and Weisgerber was elected mayor. (Courtesy of Betty McDermott.)

PRESENTING THE NEW CITY SHIELD. Pride and joy are reflected in the faces of, from left to right, Dr. Larry Chong, unidentified, Denny Weisgerber, Stan Anderson, and David Hufton. (Courtesy of City of Milpitas.) There were minor changes in the artwork in 1962, but major changes in the city's landscape were to come.

THE MINUTE MAN. The Minute Man has become the symbol of Milpitas and appears on the city's insignia.

FRONTIER DAYS, 1973. These horsemen are waiting by the grammar school for the parade to begin. On the heels of the town's escape from annexation to San Jose, the Milpitas Merchant's Association and the chamber of commerce were proud to initiate an annual Wild West celebration beginning in 1962. Milpitas had a tradition of festivals and community involvement. The association's purpose was "the fostering of retail trade, the promotion of friendly relationships among merchants, and the general public and civic organizations." The annual five-day carnival continued from 1962 through 1981, when it was replaced by the Corn Festival for two years. Today, the chamber's Art and Wine Festival has been well attended. (Courtesy of author.)

HOOSEGOW, C. 1972. Activities included an old-fashioned parade down Main Street, with plenty of horses and wagons. The Western theme offered many contests and prizes for best costume, longest beard, and even a fastest draw contest (using blanks). The carnival included music, dancing, many games, and a "hoosegow," or jail (at left). If you didn't pay up when you got caught out of costume, you got thrown in the "hoosegow!" (Courtesy of Skip Skyrud.)

FRONTIER DAYS WITH BEN GROSS. Riding the
Ferris wheel during Frontier days in 1967 are,
from left to right, quarterhorse show queen Kathy
Cardoza, Mayor Ben Gross, and Bay Area Indian
princess Sylvia Tessay. All rode in the big parade
on Memorial Day, which climaxed the sixth annual
festival. (Courtesy of the *Milpitas Post*.)

SANDY ROBERTS, MISS TEENAGE AMERICA. On
Saturday, November 9, 1966, millions of Americans
learned how to pronounce "Milpitas" when Sandy's
happy tears were joined by those of the thousands
of Milpitans who watched the Dallas pageant on
national television. Along with the crown were
$23,000 in prizes, including a $10,000 scholarship,
a new car, 60 shares of stock, and a year-round
wardrobe. Upon her return at the San Jose Airport,
hundreds of Milpitians greeted her, many of them her
classmates. They formed a motorcade of 75 cars, two
school buses, and a motorbike behind Milpitas police
cars and fire trucks. Principal Leo Murphy, who
flew with his wife down to Dallas as a guest of the
pageant, wasn't worried about disrupting the school
schedule. "After all," he said, "It doesn't happen
very often. A senior at Samuel Ayer high school,
she plans to attend Stanford and study engineering."
(Courtesy of the *Milpitas Post*.)

RAILROAD CONGESTION. Trains that held up traffic more than five minutes were subject to a fine. Commuters had to contend with both the Southern Pacific and the Western Pacific Railroads. This view looks west over Calaveras Road to Main Street at the top of the picture. The opposite view is below. (Courtesy of Skip Skyrud.)

GETTING OVER THE TRACKS. Ford was in, and the future was looking very good. Just one barrier would have to be removed. The railroad had helped Milpitas grow, but luring big industry into town created more traffic. This view looks east at cars waiting for a Southern Pacific freight train heading south to San Jose to pass. The third Milpitas Post Office can be seen on the right. (Courtesy of Skip Skyrud.)

106

BUILDING OVER THE TRACKS, 1968. The new Calaveras overpass was built just north of the original road. Winsor Street, seen above, runs parallel to the Southern Pacific Railroad tracks, and behind the old grammar school at the top of the photo. This had been the older part of North Main Street prior to the advent of the automobile. In 1870, the road crossed over the tracks just beyond the grammar school. Weller Lane and Frank Garcia's Standard Gas Station are also visible at the top of this photo. (Courtesy of City of Milpitas.)

FIRST CARS ON THE 680 FREEWAY, 1975. Mayor Joe House, Miss Milpitas Jackie Kent, and city manager Bob Brown enjoy the first ride south from Calaveras Boulevard. This new freeway marked a transition for the city of Milpitas, from a small town to a growing metropolis. Previously imposed building restrictions were removed in 1976. Any traces of the hay-makers and the flower-growers that farmed this very spot, along old Dempsey Road, would be gone within the next five years. The township of Milpitas that began as a post office in 1858 was all grown up. (Courtesy of Milpitas Chamber of Commerce.)

OPENING CEREMONY OF 680 HIGHWAY THROUGH MILPITAS, 1975. Standing above Calaveras Boulevard for the ceremony are, from left to right, Frank DeSmidt, John "Pops" Kennedy, Mayor Joe House, Miss Milpitas Jackie Kent, Senator Al Alquist, unidentified, and Angela Neil of the chamber of commerce. Four years earlier, on St. Patrick's Day in 1971, Highway 680 had been opened. It was the fourth time a highway had passed through town. The first was the Old Oakland Highway 238. The second was that the Alviso Milpitas Road (237) was extended into Milpitas from the west. The third was the wider Highway 17 (or 880) that replaced the Old Oakland Highway (238). (Courtesy of Milpitas Chamber of Commerce.)

FIRST TOWN CENTER, 1983. Calaveras Boulevard crosses over the WP railroad tracks from the right. In the middle is Milpitas's second city hall, which was replaced in 2000 with yet a third city hall. Parks and Recreation is to the left of the fountain, and Milpitas's first centralized library is to the right. At this time, the police department was located on the right side of city hall. (Courtesy of Milpitas City Archives.)

Seven

OVER THE TRACKS

Milpitas now stands within the 1,450 square mile region that was once farmland. Since Milpitas's incorporation in 1954, the population has expanded from 825 to more than 65,000 people from around the world. The valley oaks stand at the edge of industrial parking lots as a reminder of the ancient harvest of acorns of our original residents, the Native Americans. The open fields of hay are all gone. The Alviso adobe site stands crowded with several new homes, and its new roof is now guarded with an eight-foot fence. The Tularcitos adobe site remains a beautiful park, while the American elms at the old O'Toole Ranch wait to hold a new park. The old grammar school's new library is a wonderful addition. The Smith/DeVries house stands empty and will be preserved. Elevated light rails cross the old railroad tracks, soon to be replaced with an extension of Bay Area Rapid Transit (BART). One old orchard of apricots still graces our hills, while millionaires' mansions rim the fringes of two competing golf courses. A great mall has taken over the site of the old Ford plant, and contemporary barns hold a second discount shopping mart. The Kozy Kitchen and Fat Boy Barbeque are no longer to be seen.

MILPITAS CITY HALL, 1969–2000. When the first overpass was built over the railroad tracks in 1968, a new city hall (the second) was built in the center of town. It was designed by Noburu Nakamura in a contemporary Prairie style to represent a new united Milpitas. (Courtesy of author.)

CHAMBER OF COMMERCE. Since 1957, the Milpitas Chamber of Commerce has served as a public relations branch of the city, responsible for distributing maps, brochures, and postcards that tout the merits of Milpitas. Publisher and co-owner of the *Milpitas Post*, Mort Levine, was the first president of the Milpitas Chamber of Commerce in 1956, followed by Sal Cracolice, Joe McInerney, Jerry Ahearn, Ben Rodgers, and many others. "Smaller for Friendship, Bigger for Results," said Gaye Morando in 2004. The chamber's logo accurately depicts the history of Milpitas. It was designed in 1980 by Ron G. Wayne, who participated in a contest held by the chamber. "M" is big in Milpitas! (Courtesy of Ron G. Wayne.)

FIRST SUPERMARKET, 1971. Who can forget the blue light specials? At the north end of Main Street, the K-mart shopping center was built on the site of Judge Weller's dairy. Locals could now shop at one center without having to leave town. Originally, K-mart's popularity even attracted shoppers from adjacent communities, but in the late 1990s the landowner opted not to renew the lease. He sold the land for high-density affordable housing. (Courtesy of Skip Skyrud.)

GREAT MALL, 1994. Formally the site of the Ford assembly plant, the 1.3 million square feet of the Great Mall now offer shoppers the chance to walk a 1.25 mile circle in search of bargains. Recently, a go-between corridor was added. The massive sign stands eight stories above the shopping mall and is visible from a great distance. Before May 1983, the tower proudly displayed the "Ford" logo. But historically, the tower was more than a sign. Around 1966, Ford expanded the assembly plant by building the tower to provide a holding area for completed painted bodies and pickup boxes. The tower was automated to allow for a predetermined scheduled of a car or truck to be put into the trim line for final assembly. Approximately 50 cars and truck bodies could be stored within the large elevated holding area at one time. A customer or a dealership could order just the features they desired. (Courtesy of author.)

McCARTHY RANCH SHOPPING CENTER OF McCARTHY RANCH. A series of colorful "barns" (stores) are spread out from the Alviso-Milpitas Road (Highway 237), to a giant Wal-Mart store to the north. Borders Books & Music at the south entrance is the first barn in the "Barn Yard," and it stocks copies of this book and other Arcadia publications. (Courtesy of author.)

LIONS CLUB. Pictured here are "knights of the blind in the crusade against darkness." Installation of club members in 1963 included, from left to right, Charles Mason, secretary; Eddie Rood, member; Roy Hiser, treasurer; Bob Beaton, second vice president; Dick Baker, director; Jerry Stanton, president; and George Loughborough; immediate past president or Lion Tamer. The Milpitas Lions Club was chartered in April 1963. (Courtesy of *Milpitas Post*.)

ROTARY CLUB. "Service above Self" is the Rotary Club motto, and service is what the Rotary gives to the community. The Milpitas Rotary was chartered on June 24, 1952. From left to right are City Manager Dick Delong, Mayor Denny Weisgerber, and Assemblyman Earl Crandral. (Courtesy of Denny Weisgerber.)

KIWANIS INTERNATIONAL. Founded in 1915, Kiwanis International has a motto that announces their mission of "Serving the Children of the World." The Milpitas club was chartered in 1994 and provides free clothing to the poor through cooperation with local retail stores. Cooking and serving breakfast at the Milpitas's "Relay for Life" are, from left to right, Steve Shrupp, Ron Lind, Dennis Knight, Rob Wallinger, Russ Cherry, and Mike Mendizabal. (Courtesy of Mike Mendizabal.)

KNIGHTS OF COLUMBUS MILPITAS COUNCIL #5796. This is the original charter of 1966. This organization has contributed in a variety of ways to the Milpitas community, from serving Thanksgiving dinners to the lonesome and needy, to collecting funds to support special education classes within the local school districts, and without a doubt the most publicized activity, presenting the Citizen of the Year awards. The past Grand Knights, pictured from left to right, are Hernando Caampued, Charles Capella, and Lou Horyza. (Courtesy of Lou Horyza.)

VETERANS DAY SALUTE. Representatives from the military pose with two of our former mayors, Pete McHugh and veteran Denny Weisgerber. The Milpitas Veterans Park honors the city's veterans by placing the memorial in the exact center of the city. A fountain cascades from the lake like a giant waterfall and commemorates the residents of Milpitas who left their plows in the fields for the call to war. (Courtesy of author.)

REDEDICATION OF NEW VETERANS PARK. City officials confirmed their commitment to support the city's veterans with a rededication ceremony on Veterans Day which included the official opening of Veterans Park. Due to construction of a new city hall, the veterans memorial stones were temporarily relocated to a second site. When the construction was completed, the Milpitas City Council voted unanimously to reinstate the veterans memorial. On hand for the ceremony were the Knights of Columbus, St. Joseph Assembly 4th Degree Knights. From left to right are (front row) Ed Madarang, Lou Horyza, and Ludwin Indihar; (back row) unidentified Marine, William Poehlman Jr., Greg Dessel, Guy Ferry, Mike Donnelly, Ed Blake, Dany Campos, Ed Kantack, and Phil Santamaria. (Courtesy of author.)

REDEDICATION PLAQUE. On Veterans Day, November 11, 2002, a flag-raising ceremony was performed by representatives from all branches of the service. Following a solemn melody on the Scottish bagpipes, a proclamation was read honoring the memory of those who served and the veterans who were attending. A second dedication proclaimed the official opening of the new Veterans Park. (Courtesy of Lou Horyza.)

VETERANS MEMORIAL. John Pashote, Manuel R. Rose, and Joseph L. Rose served in World War I. Albert Vargas, Melvin Duarte, Melvin Garcia, Sebastian Ferreira, John Falcato, Gerald Ferreira, Herman Perry, William Rodriques, Tony Guerrero, and Manuel Mattos served in the World War II. We honor those who served our country with gallantry and distinction in the Korean War. We remember Harold E. Boetcher, Joseph Cestaric, Warren E. Donahe, Lucas R. Enriquez, Robert A. Horcajo, James N. Mathews and Gary D. Tice, who served in the Vietnam War; and Michael Mihalakis (2004) who served in Iraq. (Courtesy of author.)

CITY HALL, 2004. With several silicon chip manufacturers now calling Milpitas home, and with its substantial population growth, Milpitas opened a new city hall in October 2002 to better serve a growing city. Many of the locals, sporting their sense of humor, consider the U.S.S. *Milpitas* to be the most appropriate description because of the monumental scale and nautical lines of the building. After all, Dixon Landing is only a short distance away. (Courtesy of author.)

FIRST AND FOURTH MAYORS, 2004. Tom Evatt (left) and Richard Taylor returned to Milpitas for a reunion as the city celebrated its 50th anniversary. Both were impressed by the scale of the new city hall. The population had grown from 600 in 1954 to more than 65,000 in 2004. The Milpitas Historical Society honors their contributions. (Courtesy of author.)

Bachelor Belles

Bachelor Belles

Bernie Henriques   Velma Valencia   Adeline Bettencourt   Elvera Borges
Secretary   President   Treasurer   Vice President

GIRLS JUST WANT TO HAVE FUN. The Bachelor Belles formed a club in October 1948. The purpose of the club was "to have a night out without our husbands and to have fun." This photo was taken in the Veterans Hall. Now they meet for lunch and call themselves the "Lunch Bunch." (Courtesy of Velma Valencia.)

BACHELOR BELLES, 56 YEARS LATER. Pictured, from left to right, are Velma Valencia, Bernadine Henriques, Adeline Bettencourt, Evelyn Dean, Mabel Mattos, Gerry Silva, and Dottie Silva. These ladies are all charter members of the Bachelor Belles. The photo was taken in front of the 1910 Smith's Corner, which became Campbell's Corner in 1954, Ola's Aprilia Corner in 2004, and at press time was up for sale for more than $1 million. (Courtesy of author.)

GREEN THUMB CLUB. The landscaping around Sunnyhills, Milford Homes, Sylvan Gardens, the Manor, Parktown, and the Pines was cultivated by many of the new homeowners themselves. The Green Thumbs is the name they have used for years. They're constantly watering, pruning, using their shears, and have done great things to beautify this city. Pictured, from left to right, are Lahoma Bunnell, Pat Velasco, Mabel Mattos, Mareila Ogle, Helen Terra, and Ruth McGadden. (Courtesy of Nathan D. Souza.)

GOLDEN HILL ART ASSOCIATION, 1972. Longtime director Harriet McGuire stated, "We promote art education and instruction and foster an appreciation of fine arts and crafts." Pictured kneeling is Ann Fernandez. Standing, from left to right, are Harriet McGuire, Joan Moran, Pat Decker, and Suzanne Morris. (Courtesy of Phil Nelson and the *Milpitas Post*.)

DICK VALENCIA, 1940. Sal Cracolice remembers the baseball teams that played at Alms Field, next to the large elms at the southern end of town. Joe Stemel and Auston Pelton were a couple of the managers of the Milpitas team when Sal played second or third base in the late 1920s. "We won more than we lost. Every Sunday afternoon the whole town would be there to see the team play San Jose, Berryessa, Santa Clara, or any of the area teams." (Courtesy of Velma Valencia.)

MILPITAS ACORNS, 1930. Each player was sponsored by a different merchant so the whole town would be involved. Pictured, from left to right, are (kneeling) Ace Miller, Alfred Carlo, Manuel Vierra, Sal Cracolice, Joseph (Dick) Carlo, Johnny Carlo, and Joe Simas; (standing) Willie ?, Vic Soares, Al Harker, Chris Scamboti, Harry Kanamotto, Frank "Pop" Valencia, Manuel Rose, Joe Stemel (hat), and Clyde Stemel (bat boy). (Courtesy of Velma Valencia.)

CHARLIE SILVERA. "I can remember as a kid chasing foul balls across Main Street when we played ball at the Alms field between the elm trees and Penitencia Creek." Charlie Silvera was raised playing baseball in Milpitas in the late 1920s. Later, his father moved to San Francisco where Charlie continued to play and meet good coaches and players. At Saint Ignacio's High School, Charlie's career blossomed and he was asked to sign a contract with the New York Yankees. There, Charlie had the opportunity to play with several of baseball's most legendary players like Yogi Berra, Joe DiMaggio, Mickey Mantle, Hank Bauer, and Casey Stengel. During his remarkable baseball career, Charlie earned eight World Series rings. Charlie was the backup catcher for Yogi Berra, and later became a major-league scout.

PAUL ZUVELLA. Playing in the major leagues was more than a fantasy for Paul Zuvella. Paul attended Samuel Ayer High School and graduated in 1976. After an ALL-PAC-10 year at Stanford University, Paul was signed to the Atlanta Braves in 1980, where he was Atlanta's Minor League Player of the Year with a .303 batting average. Traded to the New York Yankees in 1986, Paul played professionally for 12 years and coached and managed for 7 years with the Colorado Rockies. Paul remembers, "My summers in Milpitas were spent playing lob ball and working on the field near Rancho School. We took pride playing, and we honored baseball by grooming that field to be the best place that it could be." (Courtesy of Paul Zuvella.)

AL WOOL, 1918–1999. Rancher, filmmaker, and president of the Santa Clara chapter of the Audubon Society for 20 years, Al Wool was an authority on California's wildlife. Growing up on a mountain ranch just behind Monument Peak had a profound influence on Al's life. At the age of 10, he discovered and climbed to his first eagle's nest. Later, Al developed a great passion for photography and filmmaking. Hunting with his camera, Al honed his eye on nature, creating films and photographs about the wildlife that was all around him. After earning a degree in natural science at Stanford University in 1942, Al's nature photography and films were well received at numerous exhibitions and guest speaking engagements all across the country. In 1960, he purchased another ranch in La Honda and was part owner of the Spring Valley Golf Course until it was sold in 1964. (Courtesy of Milpitas Historical Society.)

GOLDEN EAGLE. The golden eagle was photographed for Al Wool's film *Ranch and Range.* "Golden eagles look down over the city of Milpitas every day, hunting for ground squirrels in the hayfields," said Al Wool. "You can see one anytime by parking on Weller Road and watching for 12 to 20 minutes." Recognizing a golden eagle can be a challenge because they can be mistaken for hawks, although an adult is considerably larger. Nests are built on rocky crags or cliff faces, although they will occasionally build a nest in a tree, often returning annually to the same nest. The nests are sometimes occupied for generations. Females lay one to three eggs, once a year. Most males do not share in the 41 to 45 days of egg incubation, but will bring food to the female. Parents share the responsibilities of raising the young. Most of its prey is taken on the ground: mammals, such as foxes, rabbits, and hares. But large birds, such as geese and cranes, are occasionally struck in mid-air. Golden eagles are protected through the United States Fish and Wildlife Service. It is important to note that collecting feathers or any eagle parts is a felony punishable with severe fines and possible jail time. (Courtesy of author.)

VIEW FROM MONUMENT PEAK. This spectacular vista looks southwest back to the center of Milpitas below. Highway 680 creates a diagonal line above, with Jacklin Road on the right edge. The mountain ranch first owned by J.R. Weller and then by the Wool family is seen in the middle. Four small schoolhouses supported the Portuguese farmers who worked the "breadbasket" within these this elevated valleys at 2,000 feet. Two hundred years ago, the valley was undeveloped, and hillside farming was essential. There are many remarkable rock fences. One is visible at the bottom of this photograph. (Courtesy of author.)

LIVING AT THE TOP OF MILPITAS. Ruth Wool Savage, seen at right, recalls, "The wildlife was all around us on the mountain ranch. We were very fortunate that Pappa [Sandy Wool] was able to rent the ranch from the San Francisco Water Company. There we had lots of deer. One little fawn became a pet." On the ranch, sisters Betty and Ruth and brothers Justin, Al, and Ernie all remembered turning an empty upstairs room into a hospital for injured birds. Today, the old ranch house and barn are gone but the trees are larger and the spring continues to run, just as it had when J.R. Weller owned the ranch in the 1880s. (Courtesy of Ruth Savage.)

SANDY WOOL LAKE. Since 1964, this 1,539-acre county park, located within the Laguna Valley in the east foothills of Milpitas, seems to have remained one of the best-kept secrets in the area. Honoring local supervisor Sandy Wool, who farmed the Calaveras Valley in the early 1900s, Ed Levin Park sports two lakes, fishing, hiking, horseback riding, and hang gliding. Spring Valley Golf Course, opened in 1954, is situated in the middle of the park. Sandy Wool was a county supervisor from 1937 to 1958. The lake was dedicated to him in 1968.

SPRING VALLEY LAKE, ED R. LEVIN COUNTY PARK. Supervisor Ed Levin was a geologist, explorer, teacher, boxer, and was known as "Big Ed." His grassroots political leadership was instrumental in creating the original network of regional parks. He persuaded the county to take over land from the state to create parks.

ADRIAN HATFIELD, 1914–1995. This master aerial photographer exposed more than 10,000 negatives, producing one of the earliest and largest film archives of the entire San Francisco Bay Area. These are part of our Milpitas heritage. During research for this book, a large flat box was discovered in the Milpitas Historical Society archives. The box was full of vintage copies of the *Star* and of the *Milpitas Post*, but at the bottom of the box was an original 18- by 24-inch vintage print that now appears on page two of this book. The name "Adrian Hatfield" was embossed into the corner of the print. The box had been a gift to the historical society from Tom Evatt, who had purchased the photo in 1950 because he knew its value. Evatt was the first mayor of the town. (Courtesy of Ben Hatfield.)

GLIDING OVER ED LEVIN PARK, 1971. Aviation history was made in Milpitas when in 1971, David Killbourne of Palo Alto performed the first foot-launched hang glide flight southeast of Sandy Wool lake, where he glided 100 feet in 30 seconds. Francis Ragallo, a retired NASA engineer, first designed the Ragallo Wing based upon a steerable recovery system for the Gemini Space Program. The possibilities of a single-man version of the Ragallo Wing were noted, and the modern sport of hang gliding was born. (Courtesy of Pat Denevan.)

MILPITAS POST. The *Post* began February 3, 1955, as a family business run out of a rented house with a desk in the living room, and a darkroom and press on the back side of the house. The Levines rented a house right on the corner, where Alviso Road ends at the Oakland Highway. From that location at the center of town, Mort and Elaine became good listeners, and they learned by doing. With lights, a camera, and lots of action, their contribution to the city's heritage is profound. Many of the pictures displayed in this book are from the *Milpitas Post*. Although he is retired, it is good to know that Mort keeps an eye on the copy, and will be sure to add his expertise to maintain the quality of the newspaper that informed Milpitas throughout the years. (Courtesy of Rob Devincenzi.)

MORT AND ELAINE LEVINE. Mort remembers his old Graphlex press camera that was used to take the first photographs for the *Milpitas Post*. He also remembers the smell of the developing fluid and the hypo-fix, and he was glad to be blessed with a number of apprentice photographers who took over the fix! In 1960, *Life Magazine* was getting the attention of the American public with intimate images captured for the first time on 35mm small-format cameras. Photography was changing, as the smaller cameras were being accepted as a legitimate tool for journalism. Mort was quick to apply this new trend to his newspaper business, and with a simplified layout, was able to offer his customers an alternative to the larger traditional newspapers. Staff photographer Phil Nelson was instrumental in this innovation, and his talented eye was most prevalent throughout the 1960s and 1970s. (Courtesy of author.)

Charter members of the
Milpitas Historical Society
were, clockwise from
bottom left, Pat Loomis,
Ed Cavallini, Bob
McGuire, Leo Murphy,
and Elaine Levine.

MILPITAS HISTORICAL SOCIETY. Milpitas's parks and recreation director Bob McGuire recalls that, in 1980, "Elaine Levine, co-publisher of the *Milpitas Post*, asked myself, school superintendent Leo Murphy, and librarian Ed Cavallini to join her for lunch, and before we left she had us convinced that Milpitas should form a historical society to maintain our heritage." Shown below are two local historians who are instrumental to the work of the society and the heritage of Milpitas. Velma Valencia is at left, and Mabel Mattos is at right. Both have lived in Milpitas most of their lives and are full of facts and anecdotes about their Portuguese heritage. Their collection of pictures and artifacts is extensive, and their spirit and reflections on the past are an important part of Milpitas.

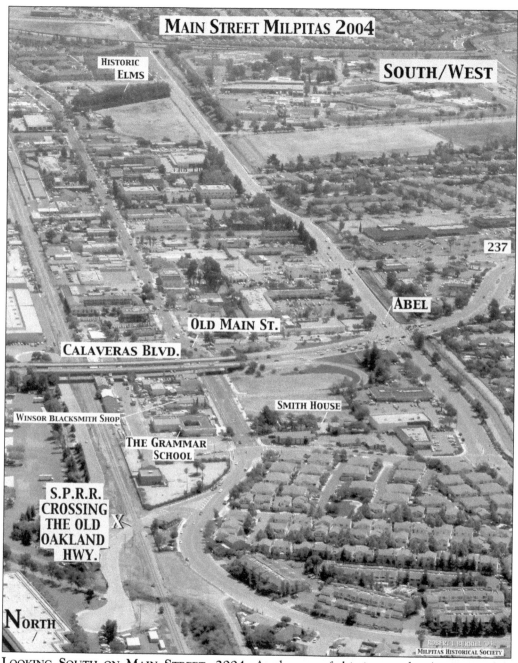

MAIN STREET MILPITAS 2004

HISTORIC ELMS

SOUTH/WEST

237

ABEL

OLD MAIN ST.

CALAVERAS BLVD.

SMITH HOUSE

WINSOR BLACKSMITH SHOP

THE GRAMMAR SCHOOL

S.P.R.R. CROSSING THE OLD OAKLAND HWY.

NORTH

LOOKING SOUTH ON MAIN STREET, 2004. At the top of this image, the American elms remain. Penitencia Creek has been moved to an open flood control channel on the right side of (new) Abel Street. (Courtesy of author.)